To Betty and Gene,
May you share these memories
as you read the pages –
S. Mary Helen Kashuba
November 18, 1999

CHESTNUT HILL COLLEGE, 1924–1999

TRADITION AND RISK

CHESTNUT HILL COLLEGE, 1924–1999

TRADITION AND RISK

Mary Helen Kashuba, SSJ, DMI

THE
DONNING COMPANY
PUBLISHERS

CHESTNUT
HILL
COLLEGE

Anniversary

75

PREFACE

"The direction in which education starts a man [woman] will determine his [her] future life."
Plato

On the occasion of the seventy-fifth anniversary of the founding of Chestnut Hill College, it is appropriate that this pictorial history of these past seven and one-half decades be made available to the alumnae, friends, and benefactors of Chestnut Hill College as well as to the broader public. Our past is worthy of celebration because as "prologue to the future" it provides a sturdy, deep, and firm foundation upon which to build for tomorrow.

The Sisters of Saint Joseph, who founded Chestnut Hill College in 1924, believe steadfastly that "on the education of women largely depends the future of society." Committed to this belief and rooted in the conviction that a liberal arts education is integral to the personal discovery and professional development of young women, these courageous founders embarked upon an adventure that would transform the lives of thousands of first generation College students and, in turn, affect the countless persons whose lives these graduates would touch.

The Chestnut Hill College experience has been noteworthy, not only in terms of educating successful women, but in challenging women to stretch spiritually. Marked by an informed conscience, a strong sense of social justice, and an equally strong sense of responsibility, the College's alumnae are women who selflessly and thoughtfully serve the needs of others whenever and wherever they encounter them. Indeed, this College has been as fundamentally interested in the formation of character as it has been faithfully committed to the expansion of the intellect. In theory as well as in practice, the College offers an education that stimulates the growth of the whole person.

Throughout the years, the College has competently and constantly shaped an inclusive Catholic community characterized by warmth, welcome, and hospitality, while concurrently creating an educational environment that demands academic excellence, intellectual integrity, and visionary thinking. Historically grounded in the accumulated riches of the world's learning, the Chestnut Hill College woman has always been prepared to engage new hypotheses and to explore emerging thought so that yesterday's wisdom can probe and challenge today's unproved and untested theories. That our alumnae were equal to this task and committed to it is evident in this extraordinarily readable history that chronicles seventy-five years of dedicated administrators, faculty, staff, and alumnae working with, for, and through women.

The author, Sister Mary Helen Kashuba, SSJ, DML, professor of French and Russian, has captured the essence of Chestnut Hill College in its many fascinating dimensions. The frolic, the fun, the good humor, the warp and woof of the extra- and co-curricular experiences present not a contrast but a complement to the rigor, the demands, the expectations, the Scylla and Charybdis of the curricular experiences of a community of learners who take seriously the life of the mind. The exceptionally compelling presentation of these vicissitudes of college life create memorable reading certain to invite the thoughtful reader to return again and again to savor favorite passages as they bring to light seventy-five years of measured moments captured in the memory of all who have walked the corridors of this house of learning, this hearth of hospitality, this sacred place, and holy space—this College called Chestnut Hill.

It is with genuine gratitude and immense pleasure that I present this seventy-fifth anniversary history of Chestnut Hill College.

Carol Jean Vale, SSJ, Ph.D.
President
Chestnut Hill College

For information, write:
The Donning Company/Publishers
184 Business Park Drive, Suite 106
Virginia Beach, VA 23462

Steve Mull, General Manager
Mary Taylor, Project Director
Dawn V. Kofroth, Assistant General Manager
Richard A. Horwege, Senior Editor
Rick Vigenski, Graphic Designer
John Harrell, Imaging Artist
Teri S. Arnold, Director of Marketing

Library of Congress Cataloging-in-Publication Data

Kashuba, Mary Helen.
    Chestnut Hill College, 1924–1999 : tradition and risk / Mary Helen Kashuba.
        p.   cm.
    Includes bibliographical references (p.   ) and index.
    ISBN 1-57864-084-9 (hardcover : alk. paper)
    1. Chestnut Hill College—History.   I. Title.
LD891.C78K28   1999
378.748'11—dc21   99-41003
                                                                                      CIP

Printed in the United States of America

TABLE OF CONTENTS

FOREWORD

"On the education of women largely depends the future of society."

This book, *Tradition and Risk*, proves the validity of this statement so dear to the hearts of Sisters of Saint Joseph and of Chestnut Hill College alumnae. The life and spirit of "college and teachers and we" permeate every page of this book. A word, a phrase or a paragraph elicits volumes of memories for those of us who have been touched by the Chestnut Hill College experience. Woven throughout this fascinating history are the lives of women and men of faith, hope, love, vision, courage, passion . . . and fun. From the beginning of the Sisters of Saint Joseph in Le Puy, France, in 1650, we are brought to the Chestnut Hill College of 1999, a modern, liberal arts college addressing the needs of today through the College for Women, and the co-ed ACCELERATED and Graduate Divisions.

We see in the concrete reality of Sister Maria Kostka's words that Chestnut Hill College "will prepare you to learn how to earn a living, because you must. But you are here to learn how to live."

For those of us who received at Chestnut Hill the gift of learning "how to live," this history of the College reminds us of the friendships, the fun, the goodness that surrounded us in our days at Chestnut Hill.

And who would be better to take us through this history of Chestnut Hill College than Sister Mary Helen Kashuba, SSJ, DML, a distinguished alumna, erudite professor, international lecturer and traveler, prolific writer, and currently professor of French and Russian at Chestnut Hill College.

Knowing many of the early pioneers of the College and associating with many students, faculty, alumnae, and staff through the years, she has grown with the people who populate this book. Most of all, she brings the love and challenge, the "Tradition and Risk," of which she has been such a part for so many years.

I hope that you will enjoy reading this book as much as I did and that you will learn even more about this beautiful treasure, the College on the Top of the Hill.

Sister Margaret Fleming, SSJ
Class of 1956

ACKNOWLEDGEMENTS

I first set foot on the hallowed land of Chestnut Hill College in 1949, at the invitation of Sister Josephine Rucker, '36. Fifty years later, in 1999, I offer this work as a tribute to her, to my teachers, especially Sister Maria Walburg, to my classmates, colleagues, and students, who are ever present in this effort. May their legacy endure into another millennium.

This work would not have been possible without the generous help of all at Chestnut Hill College, especially President Sister Carol Jean Vale, who encouraged me throughout the years of preparation and writing. Other members of the Administration and staff, especially Lorraine Aurely, Grace Haehnn, and Lisa Schmidt assisted in materials and marketing. Lorraine Coons, Chestnut Hill College Archivist, and Sister Lawrence Joseph Murphy, Sisters of St. Joseph Archivist, put all their materials at my disposal and are responsible for the pictures included here that are not otherwise credited. Color plates are the work of Chestnut Hill College Office of Public Relations and Sister Miriam R. Allorto. The College records are so complete due to the work of Sisters Rita Madeleine Gruber, Ann Edward Bennis, and Grace Margaret Rafferty. Helen Hayes and Sister Mary Josephine Larkin, librarians, gave helpful hints and materials. Friends and alumnae sent memoirs and pictures, all of which appear in this publication, either in spirit or in print. My colleagues, present and retired, offered stories and recollections that have enriched this volume, and were always eager to provide needed information. My department colleagues picked up many of my duties so that I could be free to pursue this work. Sister Margaret Thompson and Andrea O'Driscoll collaborated on the cover, which through computer graphic design traces the halls of tradition through the arches of risk to bring the College to a new millennium.

My thanks go to my student assistant, Michelle Lesher, '00, who read numerous student publications and outlined the important items. She also proofread the text, and invited me to greater clarity. Sisters Mary Xavier Kirby, Kathryn Miller, Carol Jean Vale, and Mary Rita Boyle checked the text and provided valuable insights. Sister Margaret Fleming, alumna, beloved past dean of students, member and chair of the Board, not only wrote the enthusiastic Foreword, but also offered helpful suggestions. Finally, my remembrances go to my mother, at whose kitchen table I wrote many of these pages as I cared for her in her last days. To her and to my father, who encouraged me to a love of learning, I express my deepest everlasting gratitude.

MHK 99

The medieval town of Le Puy in France was the beginning of the Sisters of St. Joseph, founders of Chestnut Hill College.

CHAPTER ONE
THE FRENCH CONNECTION

I t was 1924. The early postwar years were prosperous. The world was fascinated by the new phenomenon of Communism and wondered at its future with the death of Lenin. In Philadelphia, the General Council of the Sisters of St. Joseph met on April 10. Their minutes record that they agreed "to begin a College in September 1924 if approval is given." Their reasons: "At least seven girls are likely to take the course. If they go elsewhere, we shall lose them. We are as well-equipped as any other community. The appliances, etc., are up to today, and the laboratory equipment is fully ready."[1] Was this a sudden idea, or had it been germinating for a long time? The roots of this seemingly rapid decision go back about three hundred years.

The story begins in Le Puy-en-Velay, in the department of Haute-Loire, around the year 1650. Le Puy, a beautiful medieval city, is one of the pilgrimage sites on the route to Santiago de Compostella. Here a simple Jesuit missionary, Jean-Pierre Médaille, about whom little is known, had a revolutionary idea. He wanted to organize a religious congregation for women without the walls of the cloister, without any distinctive dress, and open to rich and poor alike. Instead of remaining in their houses, they were to go out among the sick, the poor, the prisoners, and especially girls and young women, caring for their physical and educational needs. Under the strict hierarchical absolutism of the seventeenth century, this was unheard of. Several others, such as Vincent de Paul and Jane Frances de Chantal, had tried similar ideas, with varying results. Jean-Pierre Médaille had more success.

With the approval of the local

This painting by Sister St. Luke Kelly, one of the early faculty members of the College, shows the martyrs of Privas during the French Revolution.

bishop, Henri de Maupas, comte du Velay, himself a learned man, former chaplain to the queen and biographer of Jane Frances de Chantal, he established a nucleus of six women on October 15, 1650, at the Hospice of Montferrand in Le Puy. Very likely these first sisters were not teachers in schools, but their work with orphans was certainly educational, no doubt of a more practical variety. They were devoted to their charges, and their reputation spread rapidly. Within twenty-five years over twenty such groups sprang up in the neighborhood of Le Puy. Throughout their history, their work was varied, ranging from the care of the sick, visits to the poor and to prisoners, care of orphans, and education. In 1674, Le Puy and Saint-Didier received *lettres patentes*, an official formula of incorporation, for "the instruction of girls, the care of orphans, and the visiting of hospitals and the sick."

The century intervening between the incorporation and the Revolution of 1789 was one of rapid expansion for the congregation. In most cases a school for the rich was paralleled by one for the poor. What we would now call vocational training is the story in Saint-Vallier and later Sautillieu, where the sisters established a spinning mill for wool. Here poor girls could work and at the same time receive instruction. Care of the poor and concern for all social classes has always remained uppermost in the mission of the Sisters of St. Joseph. This is evident from the early days in America.

The great turning point was the Revolution of 1789. It is filled with bloodshed and terror, and the Sisters of St. Joseph did not escape. The stories are dramatic and heroic. Jeanne Fontbonne, known in religion as Sister St. John, was born on March 31, 1759, at Bas-en-Basset, and became a member of the Monistrol community at the age of nineteen, where she joined her aunt and her sister. Later, when the community was dispersed, she secretly continued her work with the help of a few friends. In 1794, she and her companions were imprisoned at Saint-

Didier, and awaited their turn at the guillotine with remarkable courage. Tradition tells us that they spent their few remaining coins to get clean clothing. A guard told Mother St. John, "Tomorrow is your turn." But tomorrow was *le neuf Thermidor*. Instead of hearing the summons to the guillotine, they heard: "Citizenesses, you are free." Contrary to expectations, they were sad that they were so close to martyrdom and the honor was denied to them. And so, free, they returned to Bas-en-Basset, the home of the Fontbonne family, where they cautiously continued the work interrupted by the Revolution.

In 1808, a priest from Lyon, M. Claude Cholleton, was appointed vicar-general. He wanted to restore religious women to his diocese. Jeanne Fontbonne came to his attention, and on July 14, 1808, at the Maison Pascal in Saint-Etienne, he appointed her superior and thus restored the Sisters of St. Joseph. L'Abbé Piron, who presided over the ceremony, spoke thus to them: "You are not very numerous, but like a swarm of bees you will spread all over. Your number will be like the stars of the heavens. But as you multiply, make sure to keep the simplicity and the humility which should characterize the Daughters of St. Joseph."[2] It is in honor of Mother St. John Fontbonne that just about every Sister of St. Joseph college in the United States has a building or a hall named *Fontbonne*. At Chestnut Hill, the dormitory that has become home to many first-year students follows this tradition.

By the time of Mother St. John Fontbonne's death in 1843, the Lyon congregation alone numbered 244 houses, with more than three thousand sisters. The year 1836 signals a great venture across the ocean. Bishop Joseph Rosati, the first bishop of St. Louis, Missouri, advertised for sisters in his enormous diocese.[3] A wealthy woman of Lyon, Countess de la Rochejacquelin, a friend of Mother St. John Fontbonne, offered to pay all the expenses involved for the sisters who would go to America. Bishop Rosati also asked for two more sisters to work with the deaf and dumb. The first six left on January 4, 1836. Four of them were never to see France again. They were young; the oldest was only thirty-one; the youngest, a mere twenty-one. Inexperienced in pioneer living, coming from a cultured and rather comfortable environment, unused to the Nativist, anti-Catholic feeling they were to encounter, they arrived in New Orleans on March 5, and in St. Louis on March 25 after an eventful trip, close to shipwreck more than once.

Since these women were well-trained in the best of French culture of the day, their first works were education. The next year, the other two who had stayed in France to learn the language of the deaf and dumb, Sister Celestine Pommerel and Sister St. John Fournier, twenty-three and twen-ty-two years of age, finally arrived after an equally eventful trip. They began a school for the deaf; this work has always been important among the congregations of St. Joseph. Meanwhile, they established schools for girls, for boys, for orphans, for the deaf, for blacks, and Indians, without any distinction for religion and country of origin, a tradition that was to characterize the Sisters of St. Joseph, and is seen in the diversity that Chestnut Hill College has espoused throughout its existence.

The sisters did not limit their work to what was then the immense diocese of St. Louis. In 1847 Francis Patrick Kenrick of Philadelphia was impressed by the work of the sisters in St. Louis. He asked for volunteers, and four sisters, with Sister St. John Fournier at their head, set out for a three-week journey by river-steamer and stage-

Mother St. John Fontbonne, remembered at all Sisters of St. Joseph colleges, receives the news of her freedom, in the painting of Sister St. Luke Kelly.

The Infant presented to the sisters by St. John Neumann formed part of the College Christmas creche.

coach, and arrived at St. John's Orphanage on Chestnut Street, currently the site of St. John's Church in downtown Philadelphia. They met with skepticism and hostility, to the point that they could not go out wearing their religious habits, but rather donned secular dress. As in St. Louis, schools remained the main focus of the sisters' work, although care for the sick and orphans was also a priority.

Following the sisters' arrival, Bishop Kenrick wrote to his brother in St. Louis: "The arrival of the Sisters of St. Joseph has given us all great joy. They have indeed a generous spirit ready for any good work." *Ready for any good work* has become a standard metaphor for the Sisters, seen in their desire to open Mount Saint Joseph College.

In 1854, through the efforts of Bishop Neumann, a great benefactor of the congregation, the sisters acquired a property in McSherrystown, Pennsylvania, to serve as a novitiate, school, and motherhouse. In the days before trains and cars, however, the distance was simply too great from Philadelphia. Again, Bishop Neumann came to the rescue, suggesting the Middleton mansion in Chestnut Hill. The cost was $10,000. The sisters had only $5,000, but ultimately decided on the move to the property that was to house the Novitiate, Academy, and, in 1924, the College.

Sister Maria Kostka Logue's history relates their coming in poetic terms: "On Monday morning, August 16, 1858—in retrospect one thinks of it as a gloriously bright morning!—three sisters walked down the steep slope of Chestnut Hill, made the sharp turn at its foot, crossed the covered bridge that spanned Wissahickon Creek, and turned in on the rising ground to their right. There a dignified mansion was silhouetted against tall, dark fir trees; rose-covered trellises rising to small-paned windows above splashed the white walls with color; from the pillared veranda, the countryside lay open to view. . . . As these three Sisters of St. Joseph, the first comers to Chestnut Hill, entered into possession of their new home set in this rural beauty, joy and serenity must have flooded their hearts. Here at last was the realization of their dreams, a permanent home, a motherhouse that was to stand for centuries."[4] And today there is a College that has endured three-quarters of a century.

Mother St. John Fournier, the first superior, was born Julie Alexie Fournier in Arbois, France, on November 12, 1814. She spent her childhood in the beautiful mountains and valleys of the Jura Mountains. In 1836 she felt a call to a missionary vocation, and entered the Sisters of St. Joseph in Lyon. Her early formation was under Mother St. John Fontbonne, the restorer of the congregation, and Mother Sacré Coeur, a great administrator and educator, whose work was the model of Mount St. Joseph Normal School, a predecessor of the College.

Mother St. John came to America at the age of twenty-two; she was never to return to France. In fact, she spent most of her life in America far from the French sisters with whom she came. The adjustment to the new country must have been difficult. Her early experiences were with the poor, the blacks, and orphans. She is described by an early student as "grave and silent."[5] Few other early memoirs exist of this unusual woman who began many works of the Sisters of St. Joseph of Philadelphia and anchored them at Chestnut Hill. Her letters are revealing, and her best known, a report written to Lyon in 1873, describes the harsh circumstances of her early days in America, the prejudice which forced the closing of the school for freed slaves, and the beginnings of the work in Philadelphia. Her style is in the best of French prose, clear and often witty. Her account gives a vivid picture of life in America in the nineteenth century.

Mother St. John's literary style is also evident in her translations and creative works. She wrote plays for the students at Mount St. Joseph Academy, and translated books on social deportment for them. Besides the legacy of her name in Fournier Hall, she is truly the inspiration for a strong tradition of literary excellence at the College. Mother St. John also loved to discuss scholarly subjects with the Academy students, especially in her later years when illness kept her at home. She continued to teach French and mingled with the students, evidently much less grave and aloof in her later days.

Death claimed Mother St. John on October 15, 1875, after a long illness. Her last words were spoken to the sisters: "How could I ever forget you; you are my trust and my all on earth. May God bless and keep you all and each one in particular. . . ."[6] She was affectionately remembered by many contemporaries, among them Father Thomas Shaw: "I was charmed with her childish frankness and her deep humility, and her great purity of soul. . . ."[7] Her obituary calls her a *Christian heroine,* and indeed her missionary spirit, her courage in the face of financial obstacles, her wisdom in laying the foundations of many great institutions of learning and charity prove these words true.

This portrait of Mother St. John Fournier reveals a courageous woman, immortalized in Fournier Hall.

15

"Saint Joseph's House" with its weather vane
was the site of the former Dewees mill.

CHAPTER TWO
AMERICAN ROOTS

The steep slope of Chestnut Hill, the covered bridge across the Wissahickon, the rolling country side that led to what has come to be known as Mount Saint Joseph, and later as Chestnut Hill College, was what greeted the first sisters in 1858. The beautiful property known as the Middleton Estate had a long and colorful history. The earliest deeds, from 1682, trace it back to William Penn, who gave it to the German companies, the Frankfort Land Company and the Crefeld Purchasers. In 1680, Daniel Francis Pastorius was the agent for both groups. His name is kept alive in Pastorius Park in Chestnut Hill. He was a member of the Frankfort Pietists and influenced the religious awakening of the seventeenth century. He became a lawgiver, schoolmaster, burgher, and writer of prose and verse.

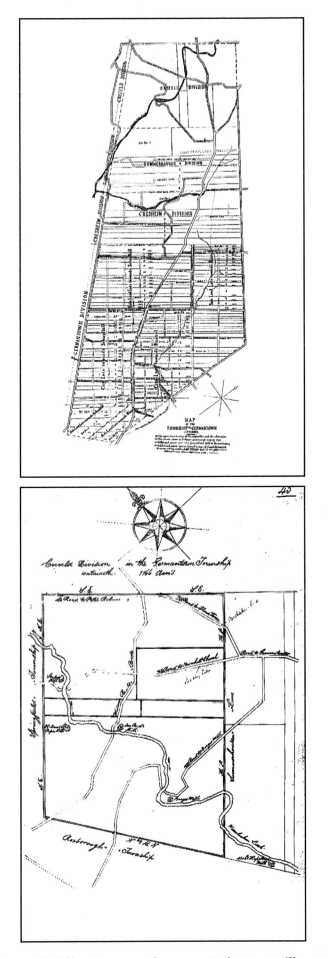

Crefield as it appeared in 1746 shows Dewees' and Streeper's Mills on or near the present Chestnut Hill College property. *Courtesy of the Germantown Historical Society*

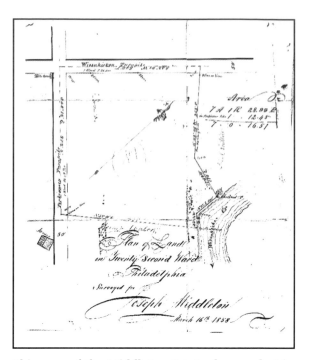

This map of the Middleton Estate shows what is now part of the Chestnut Hill campus.

In 1683, thirteen families arrived from Crefeld, Germany. They were Dutch Quakers descended from the Mennonites, and sought religious freedom. By 1687 they owned fifty-seven hundred acres, divided into three separate villages: Cresheim, present-day Mount Airy, Sommerhausen after the birthplace of Pastorius, and Crefeld. Crefeld, about three hundred acres purchased in 1702 by Heivert Papen, was to become partially the area of Mount Saint Joseph. In 1708 William Dewees purchased one hundred acres of this property, which extended on both sides of Germantown Avenue from Northwestern to Hillcrest Avenue.

The Dewees land in the area east of where Germantown Avenue crosses the Wissahickon became known as Ridgeway, the summer residence of John Bullitt, Esq., and the mansion *Monticello*, both of which are part of Mount Saint Joseph. William Dewees learned papermaking from William Rittenhouse, his father-in-law, whose paper mill, the first in the country, is still standing along the Wissahickon. Dewees built the second mill where the former engine house stood on the Mount property.

Dewees asked his son-in-law Henry

Antes to construct another mill, probably where the boathouse was located in the early days of the College. The property passed through many hands, and the Dewees' mill later became a gristmill. By 1830, it was the only gristmill in the Chestnut Hill area. Flour and gristmills, once a great source of wealth in the area, ceased to be profitable with the establishment of the great mills of the West. Jacob Paul Jones sold to Mr. Joseph Middleton "three lots of land more than forty-three acres, dam rights, said mill to keep the dam up to the mark it was in William Streeper's time." In 1858, the Sisters of Saint Joseph purchased seven and one-half acres from Joseph Middleton.

Joseph Middleton had named his home *Monticello* because of his great admiration for Thomas Jefferson. He lived in this house from 1838 to 1858. He and his wife, Lydia Barton Cooks, were Quakers. Joseph was received into the Catholic Church in 1854. Later his eight children were baptized in the home, and another born later was baptized in what was to become Our Mother of Consolation Church in Chestnut Hill, which Joseph Middleton helped to establish. His conversion to Catholicism brought much displeasure from his relatives, his former friends, and business associates.

The original property was on both sides of Germantown Avenue, from Northwestern Avenue to about the middle of the campus on the south, from the road along Rogers Center on the east, and to the Riding Stables on the west. The property included the mansion, a carriage house, an icehouse, a smokehouse, and beautifully laid out gardens on the east side, with a barn and tenement houses on the west. In 1869, after a fire in the Dewees mill, the sisters bought the property on the site of the mill.

In 1875, the sisters acquired the Bullitt property, called *Ridgeway*, a farm on the east of *Monticello*, and the summer home of John Bullitt. He gave up the property because three of his children had died there from scarlet fever; the youngest, when the Angelus was ringing. Everytime Mrs. Bullitt heard it, she remembered her lost children. The property comprised twenty-two acres, with a stone house, a cottage, and outbuildings. There were beautiful gardens, fruit orchards, a hothouse, stables, and barns. The stone house burned down, but the cottage remains today, known earlier as Flannigan's, then Father Casey's house, and now Neumann house. Saint Joseph's Hall, Fournier, Fontbonne, Logue Library, the parking lot, and the present tennis courts are all on the former Bullitt estate.

Shortly after, the Butcher property, the lowlands which were then beyond the Wissahickon and later became the first tennis courts were added. In 1867 the City of Philadelphia asked the sisters to sell the land west of Germantown Avenue to be incorporated into Fairmount Park. This consolidated the campus on the east side of Germantown Avenue, and gave it its present size, if not its present form. For if anything is consistent at Chestnut Hill, it is changing space.

This brief story of Chestnut Hill's American roots comes mainly from the unpublished research of Sister Marie de Sales Smith, a graduate of Mount Saint Joseph Academy in 1904. She concludes: "These are the lands that make up our campus and these are the people who have traversed these lands. To browse through the 'Deed Box' of the Mount is to make a delightful journey through the social and economic life of early Chestnut Hill. Gentlemen and yeomen, silversmiths and iron merchants, engravers and joiners, wheelwrights and farmers, spinsters and widows, wives and children meet and mingle in the affairs of the day. . . . As we write of these lands, of the people who in the long ago called them their own, we bring to mind the pioneer sisters who with foresight, courage and trust in Divine Providence, bought land and built so solidly for those who today reap the fruit of their labor and sacrifice. We salute them, we bless them and pray that we may be

worthy of them."[8]

The American roots of the College also grow through its educational endeavors on the property of Mount Saint Joseph. There are three main currents: Mount Saint Joseph Academy, Mount Saint Joseph Collegiate Institute, and Mount Saint Joseph Normal School. When the College began officially after only five months of direct planning, from April to September, it was not a new idea. It had grown and developed for almost seventy-five years in education, particularly in the education of women and young girls.

When the sisters arrived at *Monticello* in 1858, they immediately opened a boarding school. Classes began on October 4 and lasted until July. The cost was $135 per term. Classes for the twenty-one pupils were held in the parlor across from the Chapel. The pupils came from as far away as New Orleans, Newfoundland, and Virginia, and as locally as the Middleton children who now attended school in their former home. One of them, Ellen Ritchie, became the grandmother of two early graduates of the college: Helen Rowland, '29, and Irene Rowland, '31.[9] Helen was to write the College Song.

Chestnut Hill College has always traced its origins back to 1871, and to the Charter given to the "Corporation known as the Sisters of Saint Joseph in the city of Philadelphia, devoted to the education of youth and other charitable works . . . to enjoy and be entitled to all the privileges and exemptions enjoyed by all Institutions, Schools, academies, Colleges and universities in the said City of Philadelphia in which are to be taught the elementary branches of education and such sciences, arts, and ancient and modern languages and other literary pursuits . . . that the corporation and managers of the said society shall have power to confer such literary degrees, honors, and diplomas as are usually granted by academies and universities upon such pupils as shall have completed in a satisfactory manner the prescribed course of studies."[10] This Charter is mentioned for the first time in the 1897 Catalogue of Mount Saint Joseph Academy, stating the interest shown in the higher education of Catholic girls: "By our charter the Academy enjoys all the rights and privileges of the first Collegiate Institutes in the State."[11]

Meanwhile Mother Clement Lannen, then superior-general, and beloved teacher at the Academy, planned a Collegiate Institute. Her name remains in Clement Hall, the classroom wing of Fournier. Sister St. Ephrem Sneeringer was directress. The cornerstone was laid on April 26, 1900. The building proceeded as planned. Then came a shock: "On the night of November 20, 1900, the quiet of Chestnut Hill was broken by the sudden collapse of the whole building. Portion by portion it continued to fall until it was a mass of rubble. The blow seemed greater than could be borne."[12]

Worse still, the sisters had to bear the entire loss, since the contractor had not covered the operation with insurance. At the encouragement of Archbishop Ryan, the sisters sent out a public appeal through the press, on the grounds that the sisters' loss was, in a way, the loss of everyone interested in Catholic education. Money came from many unexpected sources. Meanwhile, the contract for the new building was signed with Payne and Company, for $294,000. The cornerstone of the present St. Joseph's Hall was laid March 20, 1902, and the building opened on September 29, 1903. The inscription above the main entrance still reads: *Mount Saint Joseph Collegiate Institute.*

Beginning with the Class of 1904, the first from the new building, the program of Commencement and the Diplomas read: Mount Saint Joseph College. Those who received the Gold Medal and Diploma are credited with having completed the "Collegiate Course." The Catalogue reads: *Mount St. Joseph College for Women with Academic and Preparatory Departments, conducted by the Sisters of Saint Joseph,* and states: "When in 1858 the

Sister St. Ephrem Sneeringer, directress of the Academy, insisted on the Rotunda.

Sisters of Saint Joseph opened their first Academy at Chestnut Hill, they little dreamed that, before fifty years had passed, the magnificent College of today would rise in their beautiful Valley home. The evolution from a small Academy to a well-planned and well-equipped College contained phases which added to the wisdom and experience of the Sisterhood. . . ." Graduates took examinations from Catholic University, with which the school was affiliated from 1904 to 1914. They were superior in English, though not in mathematics, sciences, and foreign languages.

The curriculum for Bachelor of Arts included four years of Latin and Greek, one modern language, English, History, Math, Philosophy, a total of twenty-six hours a week. The curriculum for Bachelor of Literature was much the same, with more Science, including Astronomy. The Catalogue adds: "The facts contained in the text-book are verified by actual observations, for which special facilities are afforded by a well-appointed Astronomical Observatory." The curriculum for the Bachelor of Science included Chemistry, Physics, and Astronomy, but not yet Biology. Religion courses in the Academy and College were only for Catholic students.

In 1905 three students registered for college credit, but no one finished. Some students later received college credits from the Department of Education. Anna Scanlan, 1913–1914, was allowed two years of college credit, receiving her degree from Chestnut Hill College in 1942. Ten other students followed the curriculum. Were they entitled to college credit? In 1970 Sister Marie de Sales observed: "This question cannot be answered categorically *Yes* or *No*. The same standards cannot be used to judge college credits of fifty years ago and those of today. There were no accrediting agencies to set standards and evaluate them; men's colleges accented the Classics and preparation for the learned professions; women's colleges had not yet found themselves. . . ."[13] The college program functioned largely as a junior college.

Meanwhile a significant document appears. The original is lost, as is any correspondence surrounding it. It is dated November 14, 1906, and signed by Nathan C. Schaeffer, State Superintendent of Public Instruction, Secretary College and University Council. In part it reads: "The announcement of your catalogue that your institution confers the Degrees of Bachelor of Arts, Bachelor of Science and Bachelor of Literature was discussed at the recent meeting . . . and the question was raised by what authority these degrees are conferred. No one has any desire to interfere with the good work you are doing, and Bishop Shanahan of Harrisburg

informs me that, to the best of his knowledge, you have property and assets to the value of half a million dollars. This would enable you to secure recognition by The College and University Council through an amendment to your Charter as was done in the case of Bryn Mawr College when the Act of 1895 was passed. Of course it is possible that you have a charter giving you the right to confer degrees and if this be so it should be mentioned in your catalogue."

Why did the administration not pursue this option? Sister Marie de Sales thinks that because many women's colleges of the late nineteenth and early twentieth centuries were tied into the Women's Liberation movement, the sisters did not wish to become involved.[14] Yet in her report to the Community Council in 1909, Sister Saint Ephrem, the directress, explains:

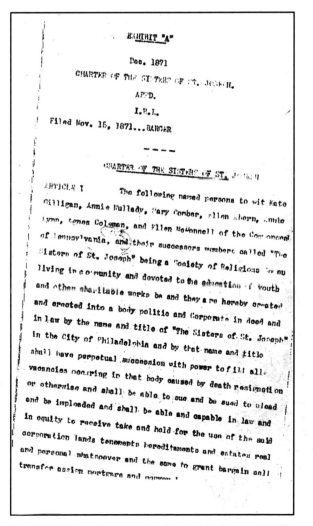

The 1871 Charter was the basis of Chestnut Hill College.

"When going into the new building, it was our intention to have a Collegiate Institute, that is to do College Preparatory work. The Professors who were teaching the Sisters the Classics at the time urged very, very strongly that we do college work. . . . As our charter empowers us to grant degrees, with the sanction of Mother Mary Clement, the school is called Mount St. Joseph College on the Wissahickon."[15] It may be that they were unaware of the letter of 1906, which has with it copies of legislation dated May 23, 1923. Perhaps there was further correspondence with Harrisburg. It seems unlikely that the administration of the congregation and the Academy/College were unwilling to take the appropriate steps. They were courageous, visionary women with a sense of business.

Solomon notes the soaring number of academies in the United States between 1790 and 1850. Many of them were to grow into colleges, some like the first Mount Saint Joseph College were "trial runs." Solomon writes: "Sponsorship by particular Protestant denominations . . . soared. Catholics just arriving also planted a few academies as their stake in the New World. Irrespective of theological differences, each group stressed activism by which to fulfill the social missions demanded of women and men within their separate spheres. Teaching became an important female mission."[16] In fact, by 1915, most female Catholic colleges had begun as academies or seminaries. In 1915 there were 14 Catholic women's colleges; in 1925, 37, and by

The Observatory, installed in the new Academy in 1903, is still in use as it rises above the tiled roofs, replaced for the first time in 1999.

1955, 116.[17] In the Philadelphia area, Immaculata was founded in 1920, and Rosemont, in 1921.

In 1858 studies leading to teacher certification were established at Chestnut Hill in the Novitiate. The curriculum of early 1860s was rich and varied. The program was interrupted in 1862 when Dr. Henry Smith, surgeon general of the Pennsylvania Army, applied for sisters to nurse the wounded in the Civil War, and again during the flu epidemic of 1916. Sister Assisium McEvoy, prefect of studies and inspectress of schools, developed an intensified program lasting until 1920. It consisted of courses, observation, and certification for specific grades. In 1887 she created a rating sheet which is surprisingly modern, probably among the first of its kind in this country. It included care of books and property, self-control, posture, voice, judgment, fair-mindedness and ability to grasp a situation.

In 1911, Mother Bonaventure Stinson organized teacher instruction which led to Mount St. Joseph Normal School, officially established in 1920. It was accredited by the University of Pennsylvania, the Catholic University of America, and the Department of Labor. Upon completion, students received their Teachers' Certificates from the State Board of Education. One thousand sisters were certified between 1922 and 1928. Sister Rosalia McGlone was the directress until 1929. Many courses are surprisingly modern,

The new Academy, now St. Joseph's Hall, collapsed in 1900.

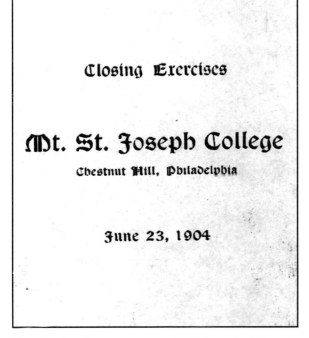

Closing Exercises

Mt. St. Joseph College

Chestnut Hill, Philadelphia

June 23, 1904

The Graduation program of 1904 reads "Mount Saint Joseph College.".

Sister Assisium McEvoy was instrumental in furthering education at Mount St. Joseph.

such as Student Teaching and Conferences, Children's Literature, Psychology, History, and Principles of Education. The directress from 1929 to 1931 was Sister Martina McCarthy.

Mount Saint Joseph Normal School closed in 1931, when state normal schools required four years leading to a B.S. Twenty-four sisters were already registered at the new College in 1924. The Normal School was an important contribution to education and to the "trial run" of the College. As the anonymous author of the account writes: "From the days of the Civil War until those of the World War, Chestnut Hill Normal Institute devoted its best efforts to the interest of the state, by training for the classroom those who had consecrated themselves to God, their neighbor and their Native Land." Sister Assisium, one of the main forces in the establishment of the Normal School, also wrote the first letters to Harrisburg for permission to found the College officially. Hers is a name that still remains alive, as one of the great contributors to education and to the Sisters of St. Joseph.

The members of the first class at Mount Saint Joseph College pose before the Summer House.

Chapter Three
The Beginnings

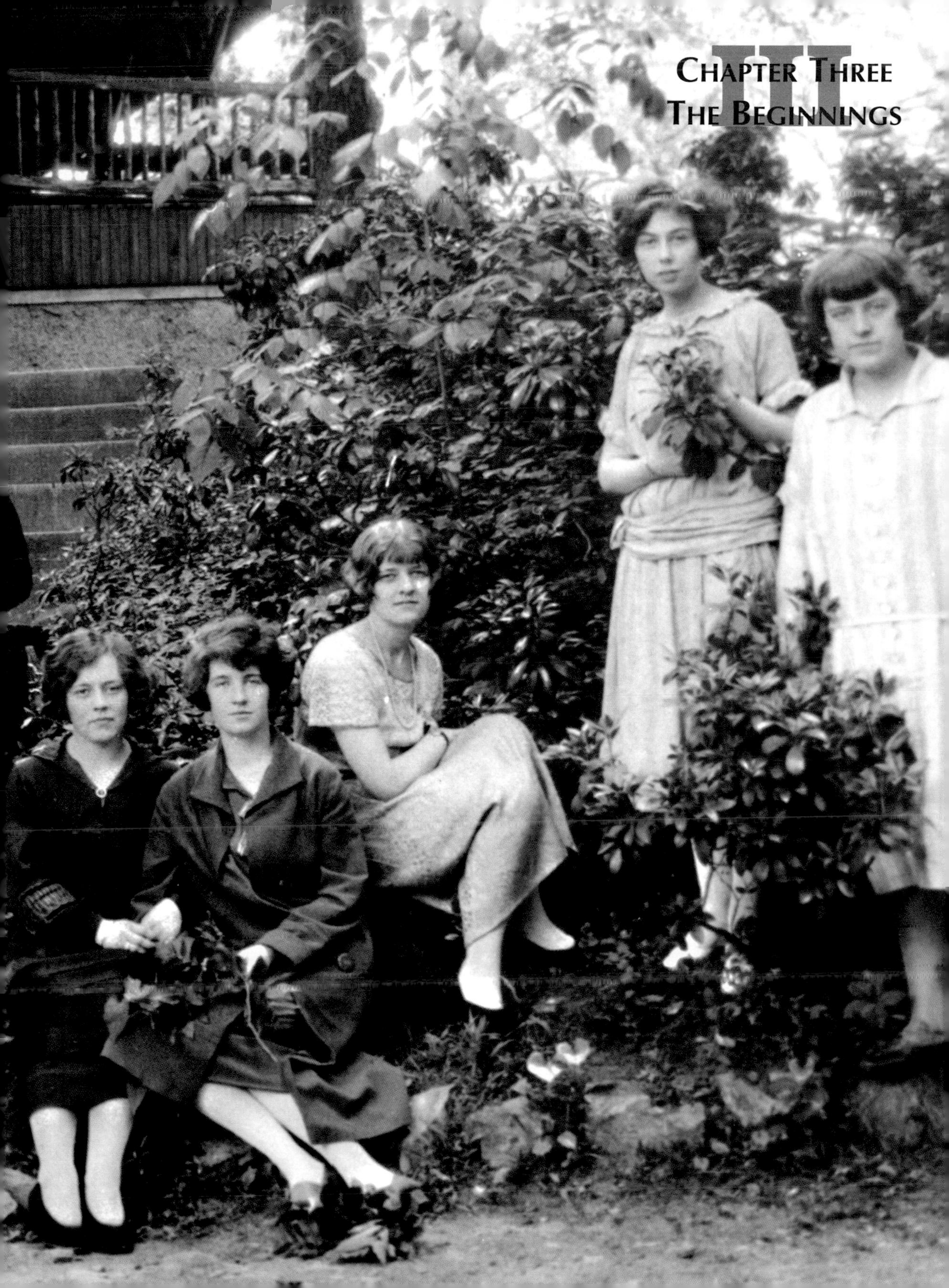

From Mount Saint Joseph Normal School to Mount Saint Joseph College, Sister Assisium McEvoy stands in the fore. On May 13, 1924, she wrote to Dr. Hoban in Harrisburg: "In 1871 we obtained the Charter. . . . As you know, we have been doing here only High School work in the Academy, but circumstances have forced us to enter now upon College work, and while we have not yet given out publicly this idea, we must push it to the fore as speedily as possible or lose out. The one impediment is that our Charter is too old, and we do not know exactly how to set about remedying the defect. You know our institution, you have inspected the equipment, you have met our Faculty."[18] A second letter on May 21 asks for a favorable answer by the following Saturday, when the Academy alumnae meet "and it would be of incalculable benefit to us could we then announce our intention."

Dr. Hoban was not ready to move that quickly. His letter of May 22, 1924, thinks that it would be unwise to make the announcement without the proper approval of the State. He recommended James N. Rule, deputy superintendent in the Department of Public Instruction, who forwarded materials to Sister Assisium. She in turn replied on May 26, 1924: "After carefully considering every detail of the Act No. 206 we have no hesitation in affirming our ability to meet at once the conditions laid down therein." Immediately she completed the appropriate documents.

The corporate title is the Convent of the Sisters of Saint Joseph, Chestnut Hill. The College title is Mount Saint Joseph College. The endowment includes the College Building (St. Joseph's Hall), worth $700,000; the Department for Teacher Training (Novitiate), at $400,000; the campus of forty-five acres, improved, worth $300,000. *Why we ask to carry on a college and the giving of degrees* states that there are about thirteen hundred Sisters of St. Joseph, more than one thousand actively engaged in teaching or preparing for teaching in elementary

Expenses per Year

Tuition	$200
Board	350
Room	$60, $70, 100
Dinner for non-resident students	80
Library and Lecture Fee	10
Matriculation Fee (payable once)	5
Laboratory Fee (according to course)	

The charges for board include heat, light, and plain laundry.

Books, stationery, and other articles are not chargeable to the student's account.

Materials ordered individually in sewing or millinery, will be charged separately.

Each student will be held responsible for damage done by her to the property of the College. Any charge of this kind will be added to her account.

Additional Charges

Piano, Harp, Violin, each	$70
Viola, Cello, Flute, Cornet, Clarinet, each	70
Pipe Organ	90
Use of Instrument, each	10
Painting: Water Colors, Oil, China	50
Vocal Music	60
Gymnasium	10
Graduation Fee	20

FINANCIAL INFORMATION

RESERVATION DEPOSIT

When accepted, full-time residential students are required to make a deposit of $200. Full-time commuter students are required to make a deposit of $100. This deposit is refundable during the last semester of the senior year.

This deposit reserves a place for each year that the student maintains full-time status at the College, living either on or off campus. Deposits will be refunded immediately if the new student withdraws in writing by May 1st for the upcoming year. If a student fails to register and/or reserve a room for a new academic year, the deposit will be refunded. However, since the deposit reserves a place for the current academic year, it will NOT be refunded if a student withdraws during the year, even between semesters, or changes her status from full-time to part-time and/or from resident to commuter.

1998-1999 TUITION AND FEES

Full-Time (12 credits or more per semester)

	Fall Semester	Spring Semester	Year
Tuition	$ 7,324	$ 7,324	$14,648
Room and Board	3,255	3,255	6,510
General Fee	200	200	400
Mandatory Accident Insurance	50	0	50
Optional Health Insurance	135	0	135
Computer Technology Fee	50	50	100
TOTAL Resident Student	$11,014	$10,829	$21,843
TOTAL Commuter Student	$ 7,759	$ 7,574	$15,333

Part-Time (1-11 credits per semester)

Tuition (per semester hour)	$290		$ 290
General Fee	$ 35		$ 35

These pages from the first catalogue contrast with 1999 prices!

and secondary schools. There are about two hundred sisters attending college or extension courses at the University of Pennsylvania, Catholic University, Villanova, and Fordham. "The expense is very great and calls for many sacrifices on the part of the Community. Had we College facilities here, some of the Sisters could pursue at least some of their courses on the premises." Twenty-one high schools were staffed by the sisters, and "From these schools we may look for pupils who may wish to proceed to College."

Was the desire to found a college linked specifically to the education of women? The Sisters of St. Joseph have always believed that "On the education of women largely depends the future of society." The tradition at Mount Saint Joseph Academy attests to this, and most of the high schools then staffed by the sisters were schools for girls. The trend of the times was to single-sex colleges, especially those founded by religious groups. Catholic leaders opposed coeducation. One of the firmest was Denis Cardinal Dougherty of Philadelphia, following the lead of Pope Pius XI. Although no mention is made specifically of a college for *women*, this deci-

sion follows the tradition and the ideas of the times.

Dr. Rule was cautious. On May 29, 1924, he replied to Sister Assisium: "The request can be acted upon only after a careful field investigation of the nature of the physical plant and equipment, the character of the work of instruction, and the amount of financial endowment. . . . With almost fifty colleges now in Pennsylvania, the State Council scrutinizes each additional application with increasing care to make sure that the new application covers a constituency not already served." He does tell her to assure an existing constituency, and secure articles of incorporation as a college, for which an attorney is necessary. Final approval could come later, if all conditions were met.

Next, ecclesiastical help comes into the picture. Mother Mary James Rogers, superior general and later the first president of the College, wrote to Bishop Philip McDevitt of Harrisburg on June 6, 1924: "Urgent advice of many of our friends and our Alumnae seemed to force us to open a College here, which we decided we would do in September 1924. His Eminence gave us permission." The bishop also was cautious, but confident. Mother Mary James

The College seal was designed by Pierre de Chaignon la Rose (1872–1941), an expert in heraldry, and features the legendary griffin, with the soaring eagle and the fierce lion. The carpenter's square represents St. Joseph, and the lily, the Virgin Mary. The heraldic trimount represents the Trinity. The book is the symbol of a seat of learning. The seal welcomes visitors to Logue Library.

stated their willingness to wait until later for official accreditation. And wait they would, until January 6, 1928, five months before the first graduates received their degrees. The saga of state accreditation is almost like a soap opera, and finds the next installment in Middle States and Association of American Universities accreditation. As John Lukacs comments: "The accreditation procedures . . . were unduly slow. They were not marked by any particular excess of good will."[19]

"On September 22, 1924, the denizens of Chestnut Hill more particularly of the vicinity of Mount Saint Joseph were electrified by the punctual assemblage of fifteen charming damsels—who with much addition and subtraction were destined to form the nucleus of what is today the only Catholic women's college in Philadelphia—Mt. St. Joseph." So states the history of the first graduating class in 1928. Seven of the fifteen were part-time students; the one thing they had in common was that they all left after the first year. A homesick group indeed, who recall with nostalgia their first days when they signed up for every course, spent two solid hours in one class, and held celebrations for one another and for the faculty. They played the usual college pranks, stayed up nights, and initiated "the charming custom of immersing oneself fully clothed in the Wissahickon." Restricted yet free, as Lukacs describes them,

The Art Studio on the fifth floor, west, is seen here at the opening of the College. It remains in the same location, with additions and subtractions to its decor.

they blazed a trail which was to endure.

Regulations included Daily Mass at 7:00 a.m.; meals at 7:30, 12:00, and 6:00 p.m.; and lights out at 10:00 p.m. Students were not to leave campus before 2:30 p.m. and to return by 5:30 p.m, later extended to 6:00 p.m. for upperclasses. Permission could be obtained, though not easily, for extensions. There were no limits on weekends with family and approved persons. Although these curfews might seem impossible now, all women's colleges had similar hours. Even men's colleges had curfews, and a rigid schedule. Life was simpler in those days: women did not work while they attended college; transportation was slower, and travel less frequent. It was an event for out-of-town residents to return home, and local papers carried the announcement.

The eight residents lived on the third floor East Wing of St. Joseph's Hall. Classes were on the second floor. The Chemistry lab was in the basement; Biology and Physics labs were on the third floor near the Academy Chapel. Cooking and sewing labs were at the end of the Music Corridor on the first floor. The Library occupied one room on the second floor. There was no Dining Room; meals for both Academy and College were taken on the first floor of Rogers Center, then the Novitiate.

The Catalogue of 1924 calls the new school Mount St. Joseph College on-the-Wissahickon, an institute for the higher education of women. Its object is "to form Catholic young women, strongly grounded in the faith, and capable of taking their part creditably in intellectual and social life." It adds that other religious convictions are welcome; this has remained throughout the history of the College. The early twenties were prosperous years, although the costs would be great for middle-class professional families who sent their daughters to college. The very wealthy did not go to college, but rather to exclusive finishing schools; the very poor could not afford it.

Mother Mary James, at that time superior general, was the first president. This was the custom of the time in colleges run by women religious. Sister Maria Kostka was dean, but performed many presidential functions. Most of the first faculty were sisters. Many were to remain with the College well into the future. Sister Maria Walburg Fanning taught Latin and Greek; Dean Sister Maria Kostka, English and Medieval History. Sister Consilii taught Latin and German; Sister Josefita Maria, Spanish. Lay professors joined them, and the College has always tried to balance the two. Joseph A. Hickey, OSA, taught Religion; James J. Walsh, LL.D., Ph.D, M.D, taught Physiological Psychology. Angela Gagnon taught French; Miriam Ferris, Physical Education, and Alvira Holly, Dressmaking and Millinery.

What did these first students do? Their history makes some casual allusions to class, and states that their first exams were a nightmare. Like all college students, they remember other experiences more. Some were to become tradition at Chestnut Hill, such as May Day, Christmas Decorations, and Investiture with cap and gown. Students recall "the way Miss Gagnon used to have to round up her French class every day . . . the disastrous results of our perfectly legitimate organized cut, the direful clashes with authority over seven o'clock breakfast and seven-thirty silence . . . the way we threw Miriam's clothes out the window so she could run the gauntlet of the watchful faculty and meet her loved one outside. . . ."

While students enjoyed one another and began the sport of challenging authority, authority worked for accreditation. David J. Smyth, College attorney, had many tumultuous moments. In December of 1924, Albert Lindsay Rowland, the director of the Teachers' Bureau, visited Mount Saint Joseph. He advised proceeding with the curriculum under the original Charter. Encouraging as this might seem, his next counsel no doubt disturbed the president and dean. On January 21,

The first Library was located on the second floor, west wing, of St. Joseph's Hall. The tables and busts still remain in Logue Library.

1925, he recommended that they "maintain a college faculty housed independently from the Academy and offer intellectual challenges to students." Other such recommendations were to follow from Charles D. Koch, deputy superintendent of Professional Education. Yet these challenges prompted the building of Fournier Hall, the development of an outstanding curriculum, and the recruitment of a scholarly faculty.

Meanwhile the first-year students were now sophomores. They enjoyed their superiority and hazed the newcomers. The Student Council was inaugurated "and progressed so rapidly that people actually reported themselves. . . ." Numbers grew. While the

College opened in 1924 with only fifteen students, the Dean's Report of November 1925 lists sixty-seven. It also mentions five Médaille scholarships, available to high school graduates from schools where the Sisters of St. Joseph teach. The tradition of scholarships continues to be an important tool for recruitment and the social justice mission of the College.

On March 22, 1928, Sister Maria Kostka sent a letter to Doctor Broome, superintendent of Philadelphia Schools. She notes: "Among the eight candidates for the Bachelor of Arts Degree are three girls, graduates of Germantown High School, the Misses Greeve, Dolan, and Maginn. Because of the high personal character of these girls, because of the creditable work done by them in their college courses, and because Germantown High School is a near neighbor of ours, the Committee on Scholarships has declared its intention to tender a tuition scholarship to that High School." Dr. Broome was pleased, as was the principal of Germantown High School, at the fine record of these three young women. The College would award the scholarship annually, and "there will be no religious requirement." The first recipient was Margaret Mary Brown, later Sister Margaret Rose, who made many scholarly contributions to the College and to the Sisters of St. Joseph.

Meanwhile the faculty was also growing. Sisters Rosalia, Regina, Maria Corde, and Marie de Sales Smith arrived in 1925. In 1926 Sister Clare Joseph O'Halloran, registrar; Rosa Verspreet, known only as Mademoiselle; and Ellen Rose Byrne, dean of women and librarian, joined the faculty. In 1927 Sister Regina Dolores Devanney began her career in Music; Sister Georgina Einwechter in Fashion Design; and Miriam Davenport Gow in Drama. The aim of the College was to "offer to young women the advantage of a college education in surroundings of religion and culture." Although the College was distinctly Catholic, the mission was already broad.

The Sports Program began early in the history of the College. Betty Buckley,[20] coach and Physical Education teacher from 1942 to 1977, recalls the first tennis court by the back wing of St. Joseph's Hall. Intercollegiate competition began in 1926 with the formation of a basketball team. At that time the Gym was located on the fifth floor, and during games the lights in the students' rooms below began to sway. Rivals were Rosemont and Villa Maria (Immaculata), and the first class recall a victory over the latter. Celebrations following games and especially the end of the season began a tradition in 1926, when the Athletic Association began. It functioned until 1970. Betty

Buckley also notes that the coaches have always welcomed any students, both skilled players and beginners, who practiced at 8:00 a.m.

Junior Week of 1927 included a Field Day with a tennis tournament. Winners received medals and trophies. It did not remain a part of tradition. The same fate was to befall the colorful canoeing along the Wissahickon, which flowed closer to the College until the sixties. Two canoes were tied near the Grotto, but local pranksters sometimes took them. Students often fell into the water, but this did not deter a return trip. Hockey and golf came early to the College. Four tennis courts and a hockey field were constructed below the Grotto, where they would remain until the 1960s.

The early days at Mount Saint Joseph College saw the beginning of clubs and groups, most remaining until the 1970s. In the days when a student's world revolved around the College, there was much time for campus activities. Of these the most important was always the Student Council. It still functions with a similar philosophy, that students should take as much responsibility as possible for their actions, and make their mistakes before they left college and embarked upon their careers and families. Perhaps they did not make world-shattering decisions, but in the ordered world of the late 1920s they oversaw the establishment of other student associations, regulated the calendar for these activities, held meetings with the

Miss Gow (right) directs and records a student's speech performance.

Students enjoyed paddling their canoes on the Wissahickon from the beginning days until the late forties.

faculty and student body to discuss their events and of course hear complaints. The first president was Helen Greeve. The Yearbook of 1929, *Ononta*, praises the spirit of cooperation between faculty and the classes which, they feel, has aided the expansion of the College. The minutes of January 14, 1926, record the aim of the Council: "to develop a social conscience which considers the happiness of others rather than mere personal pleasure; to develop more responsibility [we should] work on the principle: is my school happier and better because I am in it?"

The Sodality was formed in 1927 with Eleanore Dolan (Egan) as prefect. They assembled on the third Thursday of every month in cap and gown to recite the Office of the Blessed Virgin. Eleanore Dolan was also president of the Mission Unit, founded in Lent of 1927, to raise funds for home and foreign missions. The Student Teachers Club began in 1927 to help young women in the education program find jobs and make contacts. The Glee Club, under Josephine Condon, was the first to be organized on campus in 1926. The first concert on February 16, 1927, under the direction of Sister Regina Dolores, was only a prelude to many more highly professional musical events.

As Sister Regina Dolores insisted on high standards in the Glee Club, so Miss Gow led the Mask and Foil, formed in October 1927 with Jane Evans as its first president. She had successfully directed *A Christmas Carol* before the formation of any dramatic group. In 1927, to help with the College Building Fund (for Fournier Hall), the budding actresses presented Shakespeare's *The Taming of the Shrew*. Major productions continued every year, all great plays by great dramatists, cited by Miss Gow as indispensable.

Meanwhile the saga of accreditation continues. In May of 1926, Charles D. Koch visited the College. He insisted on a full four-year curriculum, more preparation of the faculty, more development of courses, and the need to diversify the Board of Managers. His main point was the separation of the Academy and College, and it was from this recommendation that plans for Fournier Hall began. Sisters continued their graduate work, many at the University of Pennsylvania, Columbia, Catholic University. While funds prohibited a large number of full-time lay people with advanced degrees, scholars from nearby institutions, especially the University of Pennsylvania, were invited for a course or lectures, among them Cornelius Weygandt and Leroy King. The Board included Dr. James Walsh, professor at the College; Nicholas J. Vasey, OSA; James A. Flaherty, Grand Knight of the Knights of Columbus; Murtha P. Quinn, a great friend of the College and of Mother Mary Louis Murphy; and the Honorable John Monaghan.

In 1927 Dr. Koch revisited the College. He was still noncommittal. In December 1927 Sister Maria Kostka attended a hearing in Harrisburg with Mr. Smyth, the attorney, and Murtha P. Quinn and Reverend Nicholas Vasey of the Board of Trustees. However, it was not to be a happy Christmas. The petition and speech of Mr. Smyth were poorly received. "Politics involved, most likely," is Sister Maria Kostka's handwritten comment. A visit on December 15 by Dr. Rule, Dr. Koch, and Senator John J. Coyle, a member of the State Council on Education was more productive. Senator Coyle was especially helpful, as seen in his warm correspondence with Sister Maria Kostka.

One can imagine the concern and anxiety of the administration. The first class would graduate in June, and the school was not accredited. The students may not have been aware of the danger they were facing, as Eleanore Dolan Egan recalls in an interview in 1985. But the new year brought the long-awaited news. On January 6, 1928, the State Council on Education passed a resolution authorizing Mount St. Joseph College to confer degrees: Bachelor of Arts, Bachelor of Science, Bachelor of Science in Home

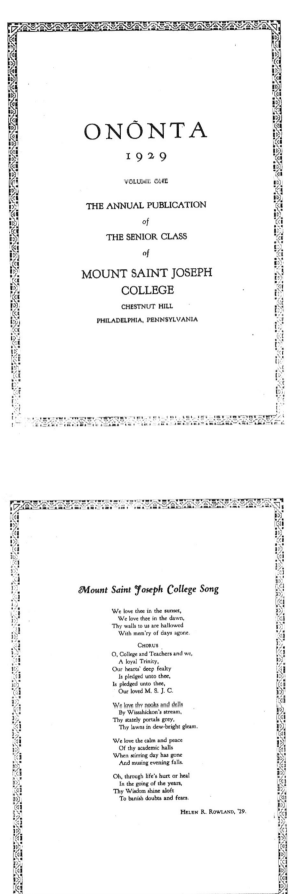

The first yearbook was called *Ononta* and was printed so well that it survives today. It contains the newly composed College song.

Helen Greeve, the first president of Student Council, is seen here on her graduation day.

Economics, and Bachelor of Music. It also includes "such other degrees as may be approved and authorized from time to time . . . and honorary degrees subject to the rules, regulations, and policy of the State Council of Education." A provisional certificate in Education and a short-lived B.S. in Secretarial Studies were also granted. The Charter was registered in the Court of Common Pleas on February 17, 1928.

Meanwhile Sister Maria Kostka's attentions were focused on the construction of Fournier Hall. In the 1934

The class of 1927 presents Shakespeare's *Taming of the Shrew.*

Report to the Chapter of the Sisters of St. Joseph, she states: "Distinct separation of building, faculty, and students is one of the most rigid rulings of all accrediting associations." There was also not enough room in St. Joseph's Hall for both Academy and College students. By 1926 the enrollment was seventy; in 1927, ninety-two. The College students spilled out to the fourth floor of St. Joseph's Hall, popularly known as Oliver Street and later Hogan's Alley. The Council Minutes of the Congregation, dated February 12, 1926, agree unanimously "that we build on these grounds a Residence Hall for the Collegians in which there shall be rooms for 200 students, Reception rooms, Faculty rooms and offices—all that will be found necessary as the plans be arranged."

Where would the money come from? The numbers of students were growing, but not enough to provide an estimated one million dollars. Since the congregation ran the financial affairs of the College, permission from Rome was necessary to spend or borrow money. It was readily granted for $500,000. It proved too little for the project, which was also to include a residence for Fontbonne Academy. A second request was approved in August to double the amount. On September 11, 1926, not wasting any time, the Convent took out a loan of $500,000 from the Beneficial Savings Fund Society of Philadelphia, payable at the rate of 5.5 percent interest. Proposals came in immediately from six contractors. The estimate was approximately $1 million. Most wanted about sixteen to eighteen months. McCloskey agreed to complete the building by June 1, 1928, and his bid was accepted.[21] On March 1, 1927, Paul Monaghan was chosen architect. Groundbreaking took place on March 23, 1927. On May 6, 1927, McCloskey, Mother Mary James, Sister Assisium, and Sister Mary Louis, then superior of the Academy and College (1922–1928), signed a contract for $1,041,208.

Mother Mary Louis took a lively interest in the rising building. Sister Ann Edward Bennis, her friend and admirer, writes: "She avidly studied the blueprints, prices, and all the most minute details of construction. At meetings with architects, builders and the myriad of workers involved in the daring venture, she was well informed, and cautious not to be fleeced by any company or CEO. During the construction . . . Mother never wearied of exploring the steel framework. Sisters used to hide lest a polite 'Come with me' meant a precarious trek through rafters, scaffolds and girders. These treks were astounding in view of Mother's large frame and crippling arthritis. The builders marveled at her knowledge of mortar and stone; plasterers and plumbers heeded her suggestions about asbestos or pipes, while carpenters heeded her suggestions about wood and furniture."[22]

Sister Rose Philippine Smith corroborates the story in 1982: "Each afternoon, after classes were over [in the Academy], she would choose one or two of us to accompany her to the college. . . . We set out with her right hand in ours, and her left hand holding her habit up. At first, the floors were not yet laid, and so the way was somewhat perilous. . . . On our return to the Academy, we usually carried back some items to be considered: two kinds of roof tile, two kinds of rain gutter. She might ask, "Which do you think is better?" If you replied, "I don't know, Mother," you soon learned never to use that response, because Mother said, "Have an opinion; you're not too young to have an opinion; tell me what you think."

Mother Mary Louis wanted an Olympic pool, for that was the very best. She also insisted that Fournier Chapel be larger, and extend into the court. She had planned its location so that everyone would pass it, but not pass it by. She wanted the kitchen layout changed to conform to the latest plan from Dougherty and Sons. Shortly after the completion of Fournier Hall,

Mother Mary Louis Murphy supervised many details in the construction of Fournier Hall.

The beginning of construction on Fournier Hall is seen here on April 29, 1928.

Fournier Hall was built on the site where the House of Loreto formerly stood.

Mother Mary Louis was transferred and seldom if ever had any contact with the College. Sister Ann Edward, however, notes a tribute to her magnanimity. When the dean of the College was to be named, she recommended strongly Sister Maria Kostka, with whom she had been at cross-purposes in the Academy, insisting that Sister Maria Kostka was the best equipped.

The conflict did not end as yet. Sister Maria Kostka had to establish the independence of the College from the congregation, a long and difficult process. The College was not a boarding school. An incident recorded by Sister Consuelo Maria Aherne shows the clash of these two strong personalities. Sister Maria Kostka wanted the students to wear their caps and gowns; Mother Mary Louis, veils. Needless to say, Sister Maria Kostka prevailed.[23]

Miss Gow describes Mother Mary Louis as "the superior of the house whose warmth embraced every new person who came." Sister Grace Marie admired her for working untiringly to have the College established, but also noted her bluntness. Dorothy Barton gives an affectionate portrayal of her, and had visited her as she lay dying in Norwood Infirmary in 1943. Her memory lives on among the sisters and at the College.

In the year 1927–1928 Fournier Hall was still under construction. The actual estimate for the entire building finished, grounds graded and levelled, and walks laid was $1,359,987.

Monaghan, the architect, strongly advised Mount Airy granite, which would cost $25,000 over Chestnut Hill stone, of which the Academy was constructed. The Convent, site of the present Rogers Center, is built in Holmesburg granite. The contract included moving the House of Loreto, demolishing and reconstructing it near the Summer House. It was erected at Mount Saint Joseph in 1897 in thanksgiving for the papal approbation of the rule and the institute in 1895.[24] This building has been the object of curiosity to many inquiring students who have researched it throughout the years.

Meanwhile, a note from Concrete Steel Company, signed by G. E. Dale, states that he wants "to make this building a permanent monument to the use of reinforced concrete." The construction of the retaining wall posed problems. Because of unsatisfactory ground conditions, its depth had to be increased, and a stairway added at the end of the building. The records and bills indicate many other details, such as the choice of Tennessee pink marble in place of white for all the baseboards. The wainscoting in the chapel, installed in 1931, was to be in oak, as well as that on the first floor.

A rustic bridge once graced the campus near the present site of the House of Loreto.

The interior of the House of Loreto has a small altar featuring the Black Madonna.

Sister Francis Clare suggested the addition of a pantry. Still the building progressed with amazing speed.

In May of 1928, shortly before the completion of the building, Murtha Quinn negotiated a transfer of funds from the bond and mortgage held at Beneficial to Penn Mutual Life

Fournier Chapel still boasts of the early Romanesque construction, and retains many of the early features.

Insurance Company. The first mortgage carried 5.5 percent interest; the new one was to be at 5 percent with a savings of $5,000. On June 25, 1928, settlement was made for the mortgage of $1,070,000. It was secured upon eleven parcels of land: the Convent and School of forty-five acres; the Bethlehem Pike property of ninety-five acres; St. Mary's Academy and Fontbonne Hall, 4.5 acres, and Norwood Academy, six acres. The money was repaid regularly, aided by benefactors, student activities, and later, the ever faithful alumnae.

The costs of Fournier Hall pale in contrast to late twentieth century prices. In 1928 the Chambersburg Construction Company charged $170,000 for plumbing, drainage, mechanical plant, heating, and ventilating. The system lasted until well into the 1960s, and parts of it until the 1990s. The two elevators in Fournier and the front one in St. Joseph's Hall, still operating in their original state, cost $23,780 total. The altar and communion rail in Fournier Chapel, installed in 1929 by McBride, cost $3,130.

More work continued inside and out, especially the beautiful landscaping done by Doyle and Company, relatives of Sister Catharine Frances Redmond, colleague of and successor to Sister Maria Kostka. They are responsible for the rustic elegance of the College campus. In February 1929, *Building Magazine* called the ensemble one of the finest group of buildings erected for any educational institution in the entire country. They note that the dining room has doors to permit the creation of a huge ballroom, and the anteroom (currently serving area) can hold a complete orchestra. The modern kitchen and the "natatorium" (swimming pool) are of particular interest.

Fournier Hall is Umbrian Romanesque. The façade and tower echo the architecture of the Church of St. Francis in Assisi. The Romanesque style, one of the richest in the history of architecture, uses the Roman arch, seen in the east and west doors, and the colonnade of the porch. The absence of the human form and the use of animals and birds are evidence of the Eastern Byzantine style. The griffin on the seal of the College is an ancient Assyrian composite form.

Meanwhile June of 1928 had arrived. It marked two big events: the laying of the cornerstone and the commencement ceremonies for the first graduating class. Yet the first class was saddened "by the passing of our classmate Dorothea Fenton whose unchanging selflessness and willingness to be of service to one and all will ever make her a lovely memory in our lives. Her love and loyalty to Mount Saint Joseph have made her spirit as essential a part of our class as tho' she were still with us."[25] Sister Maria Kostka chartered a bus and students in cap and gown attended the funeral in Trenton, New Jersey. Dorothea had died on May 25, 1928, just a week before graduation. Perhaps the name of Dorothea Fenton is one of the most remembered although she never received a diploma. Her parents, Mr. and Mrs. Ambrose Fenton, continued the Dorothea Fenton Medal Fund in her memory until the 1960s.

The great day was June 4, 1928. One can easily imagine the tears and cheers. Three prizes were awarded: a cash prize of $100 for general excellence and a gold key for scholarship and service to the College to Irene O'Connor, who later entered the Sisters of St. Joseph; the Walsh Medal for Philosophy to Constance Magee, who immediately began graduate work at the University of Pennsylvania. All of these first graduates reappear as faithful alumnae and successful women. They have indeed fulfilled Constance Magee's prophecy at the end of the class history: "The class of twenty-eight waits for the day which shall mark the culmination of four years of work and play—gladly—because it was work well done—sadly because we loved doing it. Our regrets are of love alone . . . we pioneers have blazed an honorable trail in that four years' journey whose end is now in sight."

Stone gates at the Germantown Avenue entrance still welcome the visitor to the College.

The lower door of Fournier (below) uses the signs of the Zodiac and curving leafage. The upper door (above) continues the same design, adding the symbols of the Evangelists.

An early view of the campus seen from the falls of the Wissahickon shows its rustic elegance.

The class of 1928 celebrates their graduation on June 4, 1928.
Standing, left to right, are Helen Greeve Davaney, Lucille Kahman,
Irene O'Connor, Katherine Maginn, and Marie Keffer Avil.
Seated are Eleanor Dolan Egan, Constance Magee Griffin,
and Rosemary Stokes.

Sister Maria Kostka Logue was dean from 1924 to 1942, and president from 1942 to 1954.

CHAPTER FOUR
THE DEPRESSION YEARS

The College was officially established. The enrollment was 124, up from 92 the preceding year. On October 8, 1928, the Class of 1929 moved into the new dormitory. The seventy-one residents all fitted comfortably in a building they would outgrow in 1945, when Residence Hall and the Annex opened. Cardinal Dougherty dedicated Fournier Hall on February 22, 1929. Science and Art classes were still held in St. Joseph's Hall, now outfitted with new labs for Biology, Physics, and Chemistry at a cost of $31,000. Their first remodeling would come in 1992 at a cost of over $1.5 million, $.5 million the gift of the Annenberg Foundation. All seemed positive and encouraging.

The academic year ended in 1929, the year that brought the Wall Street crash. The Depression was to follow throughout the 1930s and into the 1940s. The College had a loan of over a million dollars to repay, about $20,000 a year. Would students continue to come to the College during these times of financial crisis? Could the College continue to afford scholarships? When Fournier Hall was built and the loan was taken out, no one dreamed of an imminent financial crisis.

Amazingly, the problems would affect the College much less than expected. Sister Maria Kostka writes in her report to the congregational chapter in 1934: "It is with heartfelt gratitude that we acknowledge the Providence of God in these years of deep financial distress we have gone through. The student body showed no falling off. At the height of the depression, the growth in numbers appeared small as contrasted with more fertile years, but at no time did the enrollment drop below that of the previous year." The darkest year was 1931, but the enrollment in 1932 remained steady with an incoming

The ceremony of Blessing and Laying the Corner Stone of Fournier Hall, the new College Building, will take place immediately following the Commencement Exercises.

A cordial invitation is extended to all to attend the ceremony.

Mount Saint Joseph College
Chestnut Hill, Philadelphia

Conferring of Degrees
Corner Stone Laying of Fournier Hall
June 4, 1929

Order of Exercises

March from *Tannhäuser* .... Wagner
ACADEMIC PROCESSION

Fantasia from *La Bohème* .... Puccini

PRESENTATION OF CANDIDATES
FOR DEGREES
THE HONORABLE JAMES J. WALSH, M.D., PH.D.

CONFERRING OF DEGREES
HIS EMINENCE, DENNIS CARDINAL DOUGHERTY
Archbishop of Philadelphia

In a *Persian Market* .... Ketelby

ADDRESS TO THE GRADUATES
THE REVEREND EDWARD B. JORDAN, A.M., S.T.D.
Catholic University of America

BLESSING
HIS EMINENCE, DENNIS CARDINAL DOUGHERTY

March—*Le Père de la Victoire* .... Ganne

Candidates for the Degree
of
Bachelor of Arts

Eleanor Virginia Dolan . Philadelphia, Pa.

Helen Margaret Greeve *cum laude* Philadelphia, Pa.

Mary Lucille Kahmann . Germantown, Pa.

Marie Estella Keffer . . McSherrystown, Pa.

Constance Mary Magee *cum laude* Germantown, Pa.

Katherine Helen Maginn . Germantown, Pa.

Irene Ann O'Connor *cum laude* Philadelphia, Pa.

Rosemary Bernadette Stokes . Philadelphia, Pa.

*Dorothea E. Fenton . . . Trenton, N. J.

*This degree granted post orbit

The program of the first Graduation also commemorates the laying of the cornerstone.

class of forty-six and in 1933, seventy-three. Tuition was not raised until 1935, and then only by $50 to $250.

In addition, the College was generous to its less wealthy applicants. A letter to Sister Maria Kostka from Fred C. Croxton, the President's Organization on Unemployment Relief asks "if during this emergency your college may see fit to emphasize efforts to increase loan funds . . . with the addition of some emergency scholarships and other such measures." Sister Maria Kostka's answer lists sixteen full scholarships at a value of $650 a year, total of $10,400; twenty tuition and room at $300 a year, total of $6,000; thirty tuition scholarships at $200 a year, total of $7,400; and three postponements of fees. A reply from Olga A. Jones, October 28, 1931, states: "Mount Saint Joseph College is to be congratulated upon these splendid efforts."

New faculty came in the early thirties: Tarcisius Rattler, OSA, for German; Emro J. Gergely for Education and English; and James P. Rowland for History and Political Science, known particularly for his marriage to Eleanor Burke, '32. The new religious faculty included Sisters Anne Xavier McGarvey, librarian until 1970; Miriam Elizabeth, biologist, who had previously taught at Mount Saint Joseph as Elsie McCoy before her entrance into the congregation; and artists Francis Leo Klunk and Mary Julia Daly.

Student profiles and achievements remained high. Results on the American Council on Education Examination showed entering students from 1931 to 1937 on the whole superior to the national norm, and no basic difference in college aptitude or mental ability among all four classes.[26] They began May Day and the *Grackle*, a literary magazine, in 1930. It continued to win All-American Honors as it did from its inception; the writing was vigorous and varied. They launched *Fournier News*, the student newspaper, in 1931. It appeared biweekly, always on time and well edited, until 1968.

Students in clamoring for a vehicle of literary expression wanted the traditional yearbook, but Sister Maria Kostka preferred a publication with a broader scope. (There was a yearbook in 1929, *Ononta*, revived in 1940, discontinued during the War, and again revived and named *Aurelian* in 1946.) The *Grackle* was the compromise. It was a quarterly; the last issue, a graduation number. The grackle, a noisy bird that hovered around campus, was affectionately called Mithridates. Sister St. Esther Ryan, '32, wittingly recalls the persistent question: "What is the name of your magazine? Is it *Crackle* or *Grackle*? Humbled bird, to be confused with a breakfast food!"

In her forward to the first issue, Sister Maria Kostka wrote: "The *Grackle* will represent the varying phases of student life, but its outlook will not be bounded by the campus horizon. The college journal comes into being . . . God speed the work." The first editor was Kathleen Costello (Hehnen),'30, who began the journal "in the face of considerable opposition," indicated by a handwritten note with Volume I. No doubt the students' desired a conventional yearbook. Yet in a letter to the 1955 editors on the occasion of Mithridates' silver anniversary, Kathleen asks, "Is it not better to have published a serious quarterly magazine as representative of our student body than a cumbersome annual? We thought so then and all of you must have agreed in succeeding years."

John Lukacs notes a change in the calm convent-like atmosphere of the College during the 1930s. "The number and the quality of outside lecturers, the ranks of the lay faculty, the extracurricular cultural programs had grown by leaps and bounds. Again much credit for this is due to the intellectual standards of Sister Maria Kostka. The horizons of the kind of young woman who was a Mount St. Joseph student had opened up."[27] Lecturers famous even today came. In 1931, Daniel A. Lord and Father Garesché of Catholic Action spoke. In 1932, Theodore Maynard, poet and literature professor at Georgetown read from his own works and lectured on Francis Thompson and Coventry Patmore. Mary Dewees, descendant of William Dewees, spoke on the paper mill that formerly graced the property. Fulton Sheen, later archbishop, made the first of many visits to the campus. He preached a retreat fondly remembered by Dorothy Barton. Roland S. Morris, former ambassador to Japan, addressed the student body. Mortimer Adler from the University of Chicago spoke on art and aesthetics; publishers Frank Sheed and Maisie Ward, about their work. The inimitable Father Lynch began his long career at Chestnut Hill as a lecturer and joined the faculty in 1933. Marjorie Gullen from the Speech Institute in London became Miss Gow's mentor, and inspired the Verse Speaking Choir at the College. Many lectures were compulsory; a regulation not appreciated by all students, but they went, and later on agreed that they had learned something.

Drama flourished under the capable direction of Miss Gow. She recalls giving *The Taming of the Shrew* at the Bellevue Stratford Hotel in the spring of the first year, when women played men's roles, quite the reverse of Shakespeare. Miss Gow wanted to invite men from the nearby colleges, St. Joseph's, Villanova, and LaSalle to play the male roles. Sister Maria Kostka agreed, providing the opportunity for many artistic productions throughout the years. The Mount women also could interact on an academic, and certainly more personal, basis with men.

The early thirties record performances such as *When Knighthood was in Flower*, with Dorothy Barton in the lead as Mary Tudor, given at the Penn Athletic Club in 1932. Celeste Wills (Betz), '36, three of whose daughters graduated from the College, appears frequently in the pages of student and local publicity, first as star of *Cyrano de Bergerac*. In 1933 Richard Wagner's *Parsifal* was presented by the Philadel-

An early edition of *Fournier News* shows the beginning of student journalism at the College.

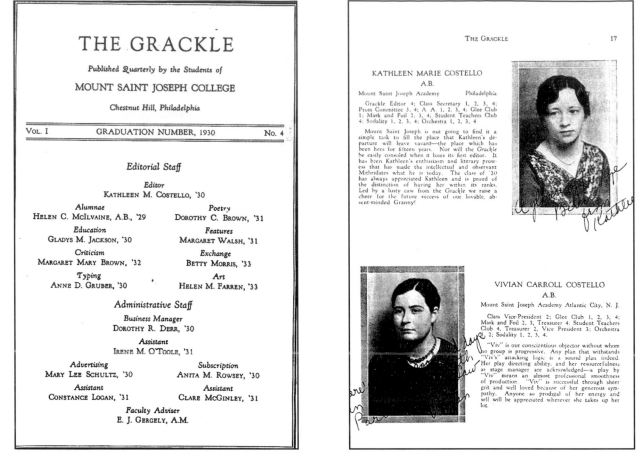

THE GRACKLE

Published Quarterly by the Students of

MOUNT SAINT JOSEPH COLLEGE

Chestnut Hill, Philadelphia

| VOL. I | GRADUATION NUMBER, 1930 | No. 4 |

Editorial Staff

Editor
KATHLEEN M. COSTELLO, '30

Alumnae
HELEN C. McILVAINE, A.B., '29

Poetry
DOROTHY C. BROWN, '31

Education
GLADYS M. JACKSON, '30

Features
MARGARET WALSH, '31

Criticism
MARGARET MARY BROWN, '32

Exchange
BETTY MORRIS, '33

Typing
ANNE D. GRUBER, '30

Art
HELEN M. FARREN, '33

Administrative Staff

Business Manager
DOROTHY R. DERR, '30

Assistant
IRENE M. O'TOOLE, '31

Advertising
MARY LEE SCHULTZ, '30

Subscription
ANITA M. ROWSEY, '30

Assistant
CONSTANCE LOGAN, '31

Assistant
CLARE McGINLEY, '31

Faculty Adviser
E. J. GERGELY, A.M.

THE GRACKLE   17

KATHLEEN MARIE COSTELLO
A.B.

Mount Saint Joseph Academy   Philadelphia

Grackle Editor 4; Class Secretary 1, 2, 3, 4; Prom Committee 3, 4; A. A. 1, 2, 3, 4; Glee Club 1; Mask and Foil 2, 3, 4; Student Teachers Club 4; Sodality 1, 2, 3, 4; Orchestra 1, 2, 3, 4

Mount Saint Joseph is not going to find it a simple task to fill the place that Kathleen's departure will leave vacant—the place which has been hers for fifteen years. Nor will the *Grackle* be easily consoled when it loses its first editor. It has been Kathleen's enthusiasm and literary prowess that has made the intellectual and observant Mithridates what he is today. The class of '30 has always appreciated Kathleen and is proud of the distinction of having her within its ranks. Led by a lusty caw from the *Grackle* we raise a cheer for the future success of our lovable, absent-minded Granny!

VIVIAN CARROLL COSTELLO
A.B.

Mount Saint Joseph Academy Atlantic City, N. J.

Class Vice-President 2; Glee Club 1, 2, 3, 4; Mask and Foil 2, 3, Treasurer 4; Student Teachers Club 4, Treasurer 2, Vice President 3; Orchestra 2; Sodality 1, 2, 3, 4.

"Viv" is our conscientious objector without whom no group is progressive. Any plan that withstands "Viv's" attacking logic is a sound plan indeed. Her play directing ability, and her resourcefulness as stage manager are acknowledged—a play by "Viv" means an almost professional smoothness of production. "Viv" is successful through sheer grit and well loved because of her generous sympathy. Anyone so prodigal of her energy and self will be appreciated wherever she takes up her lot.

An early edition of the *Grackle* shows the literary and yearbook sides.

Courtesy of Margaret Healy Haney and Mary Lou Steppacher

FINALE

THESE *hands, once clasped, are hands which now forever cling. Now have they known the grasp of friendly fingers, fleeting, forgetful of all else but kindliness and quiet love. They have felt against their flesh the strength of youth, fresh and strong in its fierce and passionate vitality. These hands have held, half-fearful, the trembling tenderness of wise and aged hands. They have shared pain and labored together and they have known the sweet, exquisite ecstacy of love. Why must this clasping be a final one? For they will live and live again and cling forever in the green remembrance of dear, familiar paths.*

◄ 2 ►

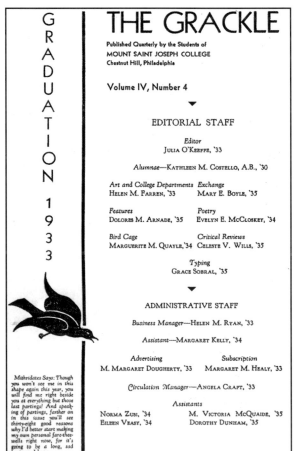

THE GRACKLE

Published Quarterly by the Students of
MOUNT SAINT JOSEPH COLLEGE
Chestnut Hill, Philadelphia

GRADUATION 1933

Volume IV, Number 4

▼

EDITORIAL STAFF

Editor
JULIA O'KEEFFE, '33

Alumnae—KATHLEEN M. COSTELLO, A.B., '30

Art and College Departments
HELEN M. FARREN, '33

Exchange
MARY E. BOYLE, '35

Features
DOLORES M. ARNADE, '35

Poetry
EVELYN E. McCLOSKEY, '34

Bird Cage
MARGUERITE M. QUAYLE, '34

Critical Reviews
CELESTE V. WILLS, '35

Typing
GRACE SOBRAL, '35

▼

ADMINISTRATIVE STAFF

Business Manager—HELEN M. RYAN, '33

Assistant—MARGARET KELLY, '34

Advertising
M. MARGARET DOUGHERTY, '33

Subscription
MARGARET M. HEALY, '33

Circulation Manager—ANGELA CRAFT, '33

Assistants
NORMA ZUSI, '34
EILEEN VEASY, '34

M. VICTORIA McQUAIDE, '35
DOROTHY DUNHAM, '35

Mithridates Says: Though you won't see me in this shape again this year, you will find me right beside you at everything but those last partings! And speaking of partings, farther on in this issue you'll see thirty-eight good reasons why I'd better start making my own personal fare-thee-wells right now, for it's going to be a long, sad business, I know. . . .

phia Symphony under Leopold Stokowski. The Mount's Glee Club was the only Catholic College represented.

Although late permissions remained basically the same, students were frequently off campus. They often gave plays and concerts in center-city. They attended the cultural events available in the area. Le Cercle Français, formed in 1929, participated in the Alliance Française in Philadelphia and went to French plays. The Glee Club recorded its concerts at local radio stations. The *Fournier News* published perceptive critiques of cultural events in the city of Philadelphia. Students participated in intercollegiate drama competitions and conferences. Home Economics majors modeled in fashion shows at local department stores. Then of course there were the dances, many in number and well recorded by the journalists of the *Fournier News*. They frequently took place off campus, under the watchful eye of Miss Byrne. Students attended the special "student concerts" at the Academy of Music, regular performances but at affordable prices. A timely article in *Fournier News* in 1933 (II, 12) notes that lack of student participation is not due to apathy, but simply because they cannot afford it during these Depression years.

Emro J. Gergely directed Education at the College for many years.

Moor Born in 1935 starred Kathleen V. Holmes as Anne Bronte, Bettina Clemons as Emily, and Celeste Wills as Charlotte.

Were students aware of the difficult years? Did their interests remain centered on themselves, or did they think beyond the campus and the city? John Lukacs sees them as isolationist in the spirit of American middle-class Catholics, interested more in movies and the radio than in Hitler's speeches in the early thirties.[28] Indeed many articles in the *Fournier News* as early as 1931 lament the lack of attendance at noncompulsory lectures and club meetings. Most highlight dances, fashion, sports, trips home, and local tidbits. Engagements and marriages were important chatter.

Yet there is another side, which Lukacs recognizes in the later thirties. The concept of social justice has always been strong at the College. Miriam Flaherty Quinn, '36, reminisces in 1955: "We read assiduously in literature and politics and economics and sociology; a social conscience was *de rigueur* then as now." Student publica-

In the Resurrection scene from *The Acts of St. Peter* the Verse Speaking Choir, seen kneeling, carried the narrative which wove the scenes of the play together. Miss Gow's notes describe the play.

tions provide evidence of social and political concerns. *Fournier News* (I, 8, 1932) urges a boycott of Japanese products to protect American industry. The Mission Unit sponsored a priest in the South, and the interclass play benefited the missions. Articles on Roosevelt, just beginning office, are perceptive; mock elections were always on target. The Debating Team addressed war debts, Japan in the League of Nations, and Hitlerism. In fact, mistrust of Hitler appears as early as 1934. In 1936 Josephine Rucker (now SSJ), spoke on the evils and horrors of war at the Regional Catholic Peace Conference in Washington. A touching story in the *Grackle* (VI, 1, fall of 1934), "Trolley Fair," by Mary Kallahan, is a plea for equal justice and fair opportunities for all. The author speaks of various social classes who crowd a city trolley, many who will never have the cultural and academic advantages that she enjoys. Other stories tell of a young man who sacrifices his college career for his family, to work in the mines, and of a husband who uses his son's college funds to reimburse his failing business.

Dolores Arnade (Morin), '35, in a

Grackle article entitled "A College Inventory" praises teaching while citing problems of the Depression. She echoed it in the 1974 Golden Jubilee issue of the *Alumnae Bulletin* where she writes: "The year 1931 was the depth of the Depression. To spend money on a girl's college education at that particular time seemed an unlikely investment, but my parents were the kind that sponsored the dream of the educated, cultured woman as the base of our society. . . . In 1931, who could set a goal? Most of us wanted to be teachers. Sister Maria Kostka met with the sophomore class early in 1932 and described to us the problems of getting positions as teachers. At the same time, she urged us to be *adventuresome,* to develop any other skills that we possessed. . . . You are not here specifically *to learn to make a living.* Sometime, you will do that anyway, because you must. You are here *to learn how to live.*"

Women during these years married later. They worked after college, as Sister Maria Kostka had said, "because you must." A survey of 182 graduates from 1928 to 1938 represented 47 percent of the graduates with teacher cer-

The class of 1938 presented *Mary of Scotland* with Peggy Gould as Elizabeth I and Marie Henry as Lord Burghley.

tification. It showed that 31 percent were teaching, 21 percent were married, and the rest were doing predominately clerical work, social service, or saleswork. Jobs were in a very fluid state; one-third lasted for less than six months.[29] In 1938, the alumnae numbered 155 religious and 382 lay graduates. Only seventy-nine marriages were recorded. There were two Ph.D.s, one lawyer, two MDs, and twelve in religion. At this time, from custom and necessity, young married women usually did not work, but rather spent time with their growing families.

The vigorous Alumnae Association continues to keep records and support one another and the College since their establishment in 1930 with the strong encouragement of Sister Maria Kostka. She modeled it on the Academy Alumnae Association. At their first meeting in the Cavanaugh Room in 1930, they drew up constitutions and bylaws. Helen Greeve (Davaney), '28, the first president, began the traditional three-year term. Early letters from Sister Maria Kostka urged financial contributions from alumnae. Money came slowly at first, but increased in more prosperous years to the point that in 1959 the College won the U.S. Steel Foundation Grant Award of $10,000 for Alumnae giving.

Although the middle and late 1930s were still marked by the Depression, it was less severe. Enrollment grew. Incoming classes numbered sixties and seventies. By 1938 the total enrollment reached almost three hundred, plus an additional three hundred sisters.

Mount St. Joseph College Glee Club, directed by Sister Regina Dolores and Nicola Montani, performed at the Academy of Music with the Philadelphia Orchestra under the direction of Leopold Stokowksi on April 3, 1933.

The Mask and Foil presented *First Lady* in 1938, starring Kathleen Reinhart. This photograph was taken in the Cavanaugh Room which was transformed into offices in the late 1960s.

Students came from foreign countries, mainly South America, Puerto Rico (then not a part of the United States), and Europe. Irish, English, and some Italian surnames predominated. Most students were Catholic, but Jewish and various Christian faiths are also listed.

Sister Maria Kostka sought to move students and faculty away from the College, the City, the United States even, and into the world. She herself had gone to Europe in 1931 and studied the English method of conducting a summer school. She attempted to provide the sisters with this opportunity and encouraged the lay faculty to travel. In fact, several were European: Emro Gergely from Hungary, Fathers Rattler and Vollmer from Germany, Mademoiselle Verspreet from Belgium, and Father Lynch from Ireland. Others were to join them.

As early as 1929 Sister Maria Kostka began a correspondence with the Institute of International Education. The first exchange student was Anne-Marie Bouteille, a French girl from Tunisia, in 1935. She appears frequently on the pages of *Fournier News* both during and after her arrival, and on arriving home she says "I spent in College one of the best years of my life." Another came the following year from Germany, Stephanie Johnen. Although her mother wrote letters in the spirit of Madame de Sévigné, saying how much she misses her daughter, Stephanie decided to stay another year. European exchanges and foreign travel were curtailed by the war, but the student body was already internationalized.

The faculty also grew: Sisters Catharine Frances Redmond, professor of Education, dean of women, and later president; Rose Martina Burke, Secretarial Studies and German; Loyola Maria Coffey, Romance Languages and later academic dean; and Francis Xavier McPeak, dietician and later supervisor of all campus buildings and grounds. Sisters Stella Bernard Gardner developed Fashion Design, and Rita Madeleine (Anne Gruber,'30), the Library. Sisters Anne Stanislaus Sullivan taught Latin; Eleanor Marie Miller, Chemistry. August P. Vollmer, OSA, was chaplain and professor of Philosophy. They were young; most held Master's Degrees; many continued their studies and obtained doctorates. They were enthusiastic and worked untiringly with the earlier faculty "to create a situation in which young women may broaden and deepen their intellectual and spiritual life with due consideration for physical and social development."[30]

High academic standards pervaded the campus. Honors courses in History, English, and Latin were introduced in 1932; Psychology and Philosophy followed in 1936. By 1933 a full Premedical program was in place. Secretarial and Library courses helped graduates toward a career. The Catalogue of 1936–1937 states: "The College prepares students for graduate, law, and medical school, high school teaching and secretarial studies." In 1937 the terror of every senior's life, comprehensives, were introduced. From the very beginning they wrote about their fear and aversion to this spring torture. The usually noncommittal *Fournier News* carried articles expressing senior panic. Yet this sword of Damocles continued to hang over prospective graduates until 1975, when comprehensives were replaced by the senior seminar which still strikes similar apprehension in most.

Students could ease their tensions then as now in sports. Varsity sports expanded into field hockey (1932), tennis (1933), and golf (1935). Competitions were arranged informally; in 1937 Bryn Mawr gave a tea for neighboring colleges to plan basketball schedules. The Mount's players were called "Mounties," and later "Griffins," from the animal on the College Seal.

Sister Maria Kostka took great interest in the College teams, and Miss Buckley relates that she had to call her after each game. Her first question was always, "Did we win?" There were wins and losses, all scrupulously recorded in the pages of *Fournier News*. Students enjoyed themselves and held traditional celebrations at the end of the year.

With the opening of Fournier Hall came a new gym which was sometimes crowded to overflowing for the basketball games, intramural or varsity. It also brought a beautiful Olympic swim-

53

International students in 1935–1936 pose in front of Fournier. Anne-Marie Bouteille is seated at the far left.

ming pool, not used right away, because the maintenance personnel did not understand the filtering system. With its operation came the swimming test, a delight to some, and a threat to others. All students took two years of Physical Education and after 1935, four. The Catalogue of 1931–1932 lists optional one-credit courses: Coaching and Refereeing, with the opportunity to pass the examination of the Philadelphia Board of Women's Basketball Officials; Life Saving; Horseback Riding; and Camp Counsellorship. By 1938 the list had expanded to include noncredit courses in Archery, Bicycling, Canoeing, Modern Dance, as well as the more traditional sports.

There were roller-skating parties in the gym, and ice-skating on the flooded hockey field, hayrides and sleighrides, folk-dance evenings, and even a fencing exhibition. The Athletic Association sponsored a Depression Party in 1931, with proceeds to benefit the Unemployment Fund. It seems that men from neighboring colleges came frequently to engage in sports with the Mount women, especially softball: "The men batted left-handed, walked the bases, and stretched the rules beyond recognition. It was great entertainment."[31]

There was entertainment of another kind in the Practice House. The thirties were also its golden years, under the direction of Sister Marie de Sales. Her accounts of its beginnings and development are filled with witty details. She had taken advanced courses in Chemistry, because she felt that Home Economics should be scientific. Indeed the curriculum bears this out. When

Sister Rita Madeleine (Anne Gruber, '30), faithful librarian until 1992, helped to enrich this history with her scrupulous recordkeeping in her unofficial archives.

Fournier opened, she requested a Practice House. She claims she was at first laughed to scorn, but was given the spot destined for the Infirmary, on the third floor. It had no furnishings, but she gathered everything from china that came from Sister Saint Margaret's cooking course in the Academy and dated back to 1893, to a table she found on sale at Strawbridge's and bargained to get for $25.

The first Home Economics majors began two months in the Practice House in 1929. They planned, bought, prepared, and ate all their meals there, on a budget of approximately sixteen cents per meal. They named the Practice House "Poverty Flat," because little meat was available following the stock market collapse. Throughout the existence of the Practice House, students claimed that their budget was far too low for their needs. They entertained guests, including College administration and parents. Some brought welcome gifts.

Later groups remained together for six months. Occasionally they had an uncooperative member, who failed to do the dishes, or whose idea of dietetics consisted of dried fruit, but most of the time was enjoyable. One of the students, Bettie Crumbie, '30, did her work at home because of her mother's illness. Sister visited her and examined her records, since an accurate budget was crucial to the program. Professors of the nineties only think they have invented college credit for life experience.

The Practice House continued to function throughout the 1940s, although the Journal, begun by Sister

Varsity basketball in 1933 featured Peggy Healy, shooting, with Margaret Kuhn and Florence Senn.
Photo courtesy of Margaret Healy Haney

Marie de Sales and continued by students stops earlier. With the war, however, other fields, especially science, accepted women, and the Home Economics major was discontinued in 1950. The collection that grew from "Poverty Flat" and included a silver tea set, a crystal bowl, and candelabra eventually found its way to other parts of the College. Others like an antique spinning wheel exist only in memory. Some College sisters still reside in the Practice House, but it no longer resembles the elegant apartment the students created on their alleged insufficient budgets.

The College seemed to have everything necessary for a prominent spot in the academic world. But the accrediting agencies did not think so. The lengthy correspondence, visits, criticisms, recommendations, and misunderstandings that characterized the application for the Charter from Harrisburg often recurred throughout the thirties and even into the forties.

The College sought accreditation into the Association of Middle States and Maryland in 1926. In 1929, a letter from Adam Leroy Jones questions a debt which is larger than the endowment, but Sister Maria Kostka lists the Congregation of the Sisters of St. Joseph as resources. A visit by George Gailey Chambers alleges that the training of the faculty was insufficient, the equipment was only fair, and that the administration should visit other colleges "where instruction is given from a strictly college point of view." One can read between the lines of Sister Maria Kostka's response a subdued rage. Yet she followed the recommendations, and on November 29, 1930, provisional accreditation for two years was granted on condition that the College concentrate on the Arts and Sciences, and more faculty get doctorates. She complied, and further updates were more positive.

This was quick in comparison to the application for admission to the Regents of New York, lasting from 1924 to 1937 with many criticisms. The faculty was weak; there is a preparatory school (the Academy); there are too many programs; the secretarial program should be abandoned; the music degree is too professionally and technically oriented; the Home Economics does not have appropriate practice teaching. What could be remedied was; what could not be, Sister Maria Kostka

These beanies and insignia were worn in the early thirties. *Photo courtesy of Margaret Healy Haney*

Florence Senn is seen adjusting the net, Peggy Healy with the racquet, and Artensie De Paolo and Kathy Igo are pulling the net. *Photo courtesy of Margaret Healy Haney*

defended. When approval finally came, one wonders if it was not because, like the woman in the Gospel, she kept insisting.

The most frustrating story came with the application for admission to the Association of American Universities, which lasted from 1933 to 1943. The first letter to Adam Leroy Jones received a rather cryptic reply that the College must have a considerable number of students who go to good graduate and professional schools, and have good grades. Good graduate schools were ones such as the University of Pennsylvania and Columbia. By 1933 not too many graduates had gone there. Roy J. Deferrari, dean of Catholic University, gave sound and sometimes stern advice. The application could not possibly be considered before 1937, he insisted, and meanwhile the College needed to equip the

Reading Room and give fewer A's. Even in those days grade inflation existed.

Frank Bowles, who visited the College in 1937, urged the strengthening of admission requirements and a better library collection, especially in the Social Sciences. Normally, Sister Maria Kostka's correspondence is restrained, occasionally witty, but a reference by Dr. Bowles to the "social class" of the students infuriated her. He intimated that 90 percent of the students came from "the middle class," far more than at a neighboring college that impressed him more favorably. Dr. Deferrari maintained that it referred to the "middle of the graduating class"; Sister Maria Kostka took it to mean middle class socially. She writes to Dr. Deferrari on December 3, 1937: "The highlight was struck when he said Rosemont drew from a wealthier class and hence, he concluded, was more highly selective academically in its admissions. This was such a patent absurdity that I went to the extreme of telling him that our most brilliant student is the daughter of a bank officer who was imprisoned in a financial crash, and that for humanity's sake we had received her in their hour of sorrow. Perhaps this would be considered padding registration!"

Indeed the students at Rosemont were wealthier at that time than those at the Mount, who nevertheless represented all social classes. David Contosta identifies this as partly due to location, since the "Main Line" was more prestigious than Chestnut Hill, and because of the mission of the founding congregations. The Sisters of the Holy Child taught mainly in exclusive academies, and thus recruited a more affluent population than did the Sisters of St. Joseph who were founded to minister especially to the poor.[32] Sister Maria Kostka gives a breakdown

of 109 out of 280 Mount records examined by Dr. Bowles. It shows 81 from the top half and only 28 from the second half in their graduating classes.

Meanwhile the harsh comments from Frank Bowles continue. He was still not satisfied with the number of students who went to "good" graduate schools. A list compiled by Sister Maria Kostka in 1938 of both sister and lay graduates gives an impressive account. There were twenty-one advanced degrees from the Catholic University of America, twenty-four from the University of Pennsylvania, and lesser numbers from Columbia, Fordham, Johns Hopkins, Loyola University of Chicago, and over forty from Villanova. With the list she wittingly observes that "like Jacob we have been waiting seven years with no result."

Questions on finances and grades further delayed the result. In 1940 it became evident that many small denominational colleges had been

Horseback riding was a popular sport in the thirties. Seen here is the riding team.

Practice House students serve after-dinner coffee in the Living Room.

now known as "rank." She is amazingly close to present-day criteria: "quality of teaching, estimated on interest of good and able students in courses, grades of students, majors, use of library in courses; increased professional preparation; good reputation and position of leadership in (the) field; recently published books and articles." To the recommendations for increased library budget, admission and transfer requirements, encouragement to graduate schools she notes "attended to." In the Addenda to the March 1943 report, she speaks of a college "whose purpose is to inspire sensitivity to the cultural and scientific values for which a University has its reason for being and which may there be enjoyed in a richer, deeper sense." In answer to the question "whether or not a college has the power to rouse and to feed a hunger for the life of the intellect" she maintains that this has been the avowed aim of Chestnut Hill and what the Association was seeking. The thirties were years of discovery, of trial and error, and of expansion. The young College was making its mark in the world.

refused approval. At this point action was taken by the National Catholic Education Association, and change seemed imminent. The letter of approval received on November 3, 1943, from Fernandus Payne, chairman, is even cordial, praising the level of the salaries, the high quality of faculty and students, and the good equipment. The main suggestion is: "It would seem to be that from your budget you might very well squeeze out a little more for the library." The Library continued to be a cause of concern not only to the Association, but also to the College, as it was even then outgrowing its housing on the second floor of St. Joseph's Hall.

Ironically, all this work for accreditation was to give but five brief years of enjoyment, for in 1948 the Association discontinued its inclusion of undergraduate institutions. Yet it produced some practical results. Many suggestions were helpful to the fledgling college, as seen in Sister Maria Kostka's handwritten responses on the 1938 report on the inspection of the College by Dr. Deferrari. Faculty should show greater interest in research and membership in professional organizations. There should be "grades" of faculty,

Fashion Design was an important part of the Home Economics major, and continued until 1971.

An important factor in making a name for oneself is having a distinctive name. By 1938, there were many St. Joseph's in existence, especially the Academy and the nearby men's college. The administration was concerned about confusion; they wanted the College to be unique. With a sense of place and an interest in the community with which as yet they had little contact, they chose the name of Chestnut Hill. At first some authorities were dubious. The Cardinal merely said he would not interfere; Murtha Quinn, great benefactor and trustee, was less than pleased. He at first refused to give his usual $100 prize at graduation, but at his death on June 9, 1940, he left the College $40,000, its largest gift up to that time.[33] Mother Mary James Rogers and Sister Assisium McEvoy signed the Resolution on March 28, 1938; it was approved in Harrisburg on April 19, 1938. The name was now "Chestnut Hill College of the Sisters of St. Joseph." Until 1945 it was called the "College of Chestnut Hill," from the Latin translation and for brevity. In 1972, the name was officially changed to "Chestnut Hill College." First of all, there was no record of the official registration in the Court of Common Pleas in 1938, and the former name was too long and seldom used.

In 1938 war loomed on the horizon in Europe. Articles on the impending crisis abounded in *Fournier News*. Japan, China, Germany, Spain appear more frequently in editorials. Former exchange students corresponded from Europe, expressing generally pro-American views. The International Relations Club studied the Austrian Situation. Yet for the most part life remained quiet at Chestnut Hill. Plays, concerts, clubs, sports, and dances occupied students' lives outside of class. They were comfortable in their college home. College finances were in the black: expenditures of $137,695 and receipts of $141,195. A surplus of $3,500 was a comfortable margin in the days when the Depression was still hovering over the American economy. The coming years were to bring a dramatic change to the world and eventually to the College.

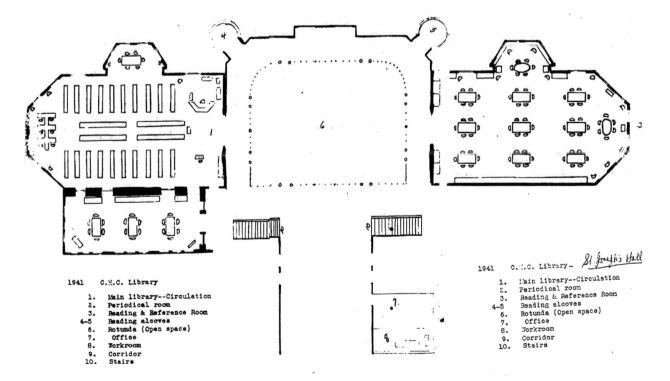

1941   C.H.C. Library

1. Main library--Circulation
2. Periodical room
3. Reading & Reference Room
4-5 Reading alcoves
6. Rotunda (Open space)
7. Office
8. Workroom
9. Corridor
10. Stairs

1941   C.H.C. Library-   St Joseph's Hall

1. Main library--Circulation
2. Periodical room
3. Reading & Reference Room
4-5 Reading alcoves
6. Rotunda (Open space)
7. Office
8. Workroom
9. Corridor
10. Stairs

This plan of the Library in 1941 shows its location on the second floor of St. Joseph's Hall.

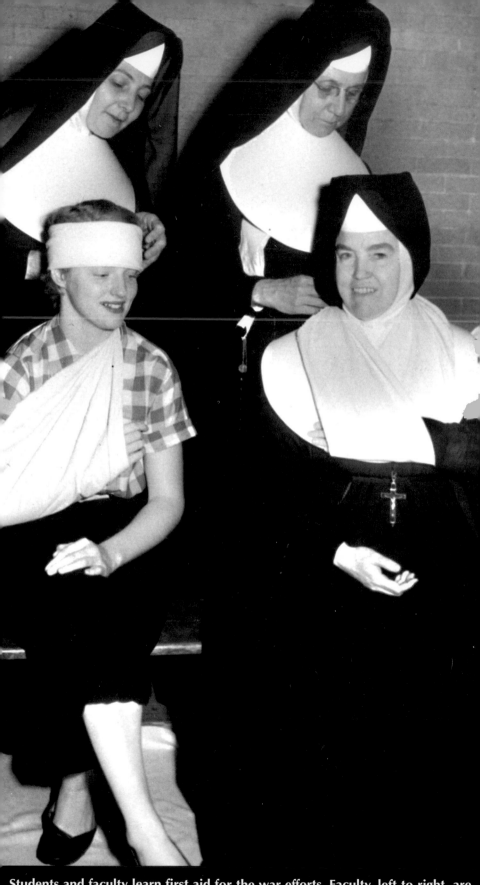

Students and faculty learn first aid for the war efforts. Faculty, left to right, are Sisters Austin Marie Grelis, Marie de Sales Smith, and Mary Thomas Murphy, who engaged in research on synthetic rubber during the war years.

CHAPTER FIVE
THE WAR YEARS

The year was 1939. A conflict was imminent in Europe. Sisters Catharine Frances and Sylvester hardly returned from Oxford when war was declared. Editorials in *Fournier News* criticize the lack of humanitarian ideals in the warring nations, and urge the United States not to enter the conflict. Any help given to oppressed nations should be done with care. The United States should help Finland, but avoid involvement with the warring nations. Keep America home!

Dr. John Lukacs reports that the waves of war caused hardly a ripple in the calm waters of Chestnut Hill, at least judging by student publications.[34] In fact the headlines in *Fournier News* for December 1941, when America entered the War, deal with Christmas and dances. Nothing on the front page reflects the milestone in history. Gradually students grew more aware of the situation. They participated in Red Cross activities, prepared surgical dressings and in 1942 they abandoned the recently revived yearbook for a Defense Bond Drive, later known as the popular Bond Night. It survived the War by twenty years, but as a student remarked at its demise, as the economy improved, the quality of Bond Night declined.

Articles in student publications focus on the personal effects of the War. How will it affect your career? Should women be drafted? Should women continue in college, or work for defense? Typical responses: stay in college; you can benefit your country more this way. Women should volunteer if possible, everyone do her share, but not be drafted. On the other hand, a very sensitive article from October 9, 1942, comments on the Gold Star for Jews ordered by Pierre Laval; the Cardinal of Paris wore it: "The yellow badge of shame had become the gold badge of honor."[35] *Grackle* fiction often raises the issue of war marriages.

The year 1942 also brought a change in the College administration, more in name than in fact. Since 1924, Mother Mary James Rogers was the

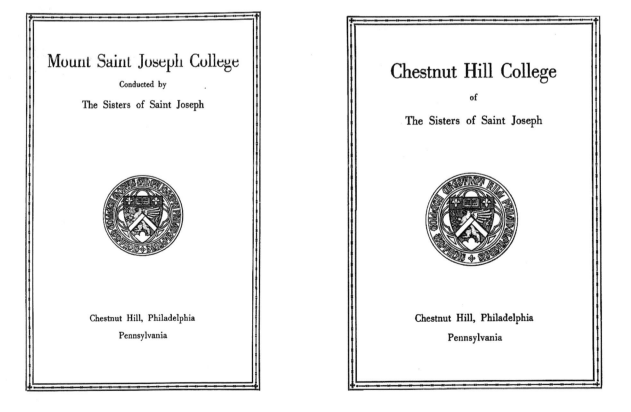

The College catalogue reflects the change in name from Mount Saint Joseph to College of Chestnut Hill in 1938.

official president, but she wisely left the academic details to Sister Maria Kostka, the dean. Mother Mary James presided over official events, and approved expenditures, often making handwritten notes on the bills. She assigned sisters to the faculty, and sent sister-students to the College. She is described as "tall, dark, of impressive bearing, with acute intuition on community problems, (and) proved a capable executive. She welcomed the expression of new ideas and encouraged promising initiative. . . . Her combination of simplicity, charm, and gracious dignity won affectionate loyalty. A quiet sense of humor balanced the serious side of her nature."[36]

Mother Mary James was superior general from 1916 to 1934. She obtained special permission for a third term to oversee the building of Fournier Hall. She then remained a member of the General Council of the Congregation, and as such continued as president of the College. Her last few years were marked by failing health, and in 1942 she died. Her name remains today in Rogers Center, once a part of the Novitiate, now housing several College offices, among them Development. It is fitting that the woman who put much effort into funding Fournier Hall should have this part of the College named for her.

Thus in 1942 Sister Maria Kostka became "Dean of the College, Acting President," and in 1943, president, with Sister Loyola Maria Coffey, dean of studies and freshman adviser. Other officers included Sisters Clare Joseph O'Halloran, registrar; Catharine Frances Redmond, dean of students; and Jane Frances Duffy, bursar (CFO). This list remained almost constant un-

til 1969, except for Catharine Frances' appointment as president in 1954.

The faculty and administration were enriched during these years by other colorful figures, such as Sisters Paul Daniel Oesterle, quiet but able botanist, and Helen de Sales Forrest, personable professor of Psychology. Miss Alice Corcoran, administrative assistant, infallibly knew what was "de rigueur" and what was not. Eric von Kuehnelt-Leddihn, though a part of the faculty for only four years, left a mark on many students. He returned for lectures, and continues his career in writing. His book *Liberty and Equality* was dedicated to the students at Chestnut Hill College.

Faculty and alumnae were involved in war-related initiatives. In 1943 Sisters Eva Maria Lynch and Edward Leo (Dorothy Hennessy) were invited to the Institutum Divi Thomae in Cincinnati under the direction of Dr. George Sperti, member of the Papal Academy of Sciences. Sister Edward Leo concentrated on physics and mathematics; Sister Eva Maria, on staphylococcic infections and on marine biology. Alumnae joined the WAACS, WAVES, and USO. Among them was Louise Bolger, '37, director of the Alumnae Association, who left her post to join the WAVES. She resumed her position after the war until 1970.

How did the war affect the enrollment at the College? At first there were dire predictions of declining college population, mainly affecting men's colleges. The *New York Times* in 1942 carried an article showing a sharp drop in most American colleges. A study of 451 institutions revealed a decline of 5 to 58 percent in full-time students, espe-

Mother Mary James Rogers was the first College president from 1924 to 1942.

cially in liberal arts. There was no change at Harvard, Yale, or Princeton. It noted that "among the well-known colleges for women reporting an increase or no change was Chestnut Hill." In fact, the year 1943 brought a record enrollment of 335 with 112 new students from seventeen states and three foreign countries. By 1945, one of the main concerns was lack of space. In 1944, forty applications for residence were refused because there were no more dormitory rooms. Extra classrooms were needed, and the Library was out-growing its boundaries.

Changing trends emerged in courses and majors. Mathematics and Science became more popular, and soon headed the list of majors. Political topics were among the frequent choices. Spanish became the most popular modern language. Technical courses were added in preparation for active participation in defense, such as Technical Drawing, Red Cross and Home Nursing, Canteen Cooking, and business courses. A course in Defense Physics included Fundamentals of Electricity, Meteorology, Aeronautics, and Radio Communications. A basic mathematics course showed the application of Algebra, Geometry, and Trigonometry to problems in navigation, artillery practice, and aeronautics. A war emergency Elementary Teaching Certificate was instituted.

In her report of 1941 Sister Maria Kostka writes: "No changes in the curriculum and no acceleration of program are contemplated at this time because it is believed to be in the interest of the general welfare that qualified students continue their education until it is clear that their services are defi-

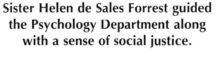

Sister Helen de Sales Forrest guided the Psychology Department along with a sense of social justice.

nitely needed elsewhere." Time proved her right. Distributional requirements were in place with twelve required credits in English, six in History, six in the Social Sciences, ten in Philosophy, three in Psychology, eight in Religion for Catholic students, six in Latin for the A.B. (but not B.S.) and a reading knowledge of a modern language. At that time there was a trend toward "free electives" in some colleges. Sister Maria Kostka rejected it. The Catalogue stresses "a balance of required and elective courses, avoiding too early specialization, and preparing the student to make an intelligent choice of a field of study." Seniors began to take the Graduate Record Examination, obligatory after 1954, under Sister Helen de Sales' watchful eye.

Fees increased only slightly: $300 for tuition, and $475 to $600 for room and board, depending on the type of room chosen. Rates could be reduced when the student rendered service to the College, or if there was more than one student from the same family. The budget remained in the black. The financial report for 1942-1943 showed total receipts of $161,189.00 and total expenditures of $159,639.79. Traditionally, tuition and fees were the highest source of income, at $63,287.69. Total salaries for lay faculty amounted to $32,640.00, a minimum salary for one person in 1999. The highest salary for a professor was $3,000.00.

As during the Depression years, the College remained generous with scholarships providing additional ones to various academies, and to sisters of other congregations. Benefactors Murtha Quinn and Reverend D. I. McDermott had provided for future scholarships. During the war years, the College responded to requests from the National Catholic Welfare Conference for students from China and Ecuador. The Committee for Catholic Refugees received a place for a refugee from Germany. The number of international students was growing, and their origins diversifying.

Nearby Canada proved a fertile exchange ground during the war years, when Americans could not freely travel abroad. Denyse Picard came from Québec in 1941, and in 1944 her father provided a scholarship for two American students to attend the Collège de Sillery. It proved to be a traditional "convent school." Although the CHC students enjoyed their stay, they were rather appalled by the curfews and strict discipline. Permissions at the College were hardly generous in those days: there was now an 11:00 p.m. return allowed for upperclass students on Saturdays, two 12:00 midnight per month to seniors, and weekdays had been extended to 8:30 p.m. The Canadian exchange did continue briefly. Later, many Chestnut Hill students, especially French majors, chose Laval University for their summer study, but few Canadians came to Chestnut Hill. Mexico was popular for Spanish, and young women from Puerto Rico and the South American countries, loathe to abandon their Spanish conversations with one another, still flocked to the College.

Life on campus showed little change during the war years. True, many trips were curtailed; lectures were often replaced by movies, much to the joy of those who did not wish to be herded to hear a person whose importance was unclear to them. *Fournier News* gave some pertinent information, but not everyone read it. Drama flourished, including *A Midsummer Night's Dream* in 1944 and *Song of Bernadette* in 1945. High quality concerts continued. David Contosta observes that most of these events took place in an exclusively female atmosphere, not very different from the typical woman's college of the time. Men from LaSalle, Villanova,

Miss Alice Corcoran discusses proper decorum with a student in her tiny office in Fournier.

or St. Joseph's joined in plays and concerts, but most events were closed to them. Since the campus was still the center of a young woman's life, clubs, celebrations, pranks, sports, and yes, even study occupied her. In 1942 radios and victrolas were allowed in the rooms, but students still deplored the lack of telephones and a van to the "loop" at the Top of the Hill. Dances and proms continued; the war could not stop this phase of college life.

Students remained concerned about social issues. In 1937, Sister Catharine Frances had received a letter from Sister Francisca of the Blessed

Sacrament Sisters, whose work is still with blacks and Native Americans. Sister Francisca wrote of "the need of zealous, responsible young women who will be so kind and self-sacrificing as to aid us in teaching groups gathered here and there in private homes, preparing them for the sacraments. Such centers are being organized now and volunteer teachers are an immediate need. The work would take an hour on Sunday afternoons. The homes would be approved, in good neighborhoods."[37] Sister Catharine Frances was concerned about sending young women into homes and putting them in charge, and at first accepted only day students, but later residents participated also.

The work, known as the Catechetical Club, began in 1938 with seven centers; nine were quickly added. In many cases, the children and adults were not Catholics, but the primary aim of the endeavor was evange-

lization in the broadest term. The *Catholic Standard and Times* in 1939 reports that sixty-two catechumens were baptized, some of these coming from the Chestnut Hill centers. These people, mostly black, were encouraged to attend their own parishes, but are assured that as Catholics they will be welcomed to the white parishes; an early step to integration. The number of centers increased, and every Sunday until the late 1960s, students went in pairs to instruct the people with zeal and enthusiasm. The project only ended when the neighborhoods became too dangerous for young women.

The sisters appreciated the Chestnut Hill students' work. A letter from Sister Mary of Grace to Sister Catharine Frances, contained a message from Mother Katherine Drexel, the saintly foundress of the Blessed Sacrament congregation. It reads: "Yes, I will give you a message for Sister, right to the point. Tell her that I think

Handwritten accounts by Sister Jane Frances Duffy show the College budget.

Concerts remained popular throughout and after World War II. Seen here are Madame Magda Hajos with the College Orchestra in 1946.

it is nothing short of marvelous the way she has trained her girls to do the Catechetical work, and they have accomplished wonderful work. God will bless her and them for this. Tell her this for me."

The Catalogue of 1943–1944, page 13, states that the purpose of the College "is to collaborate in the transmission of culture in the Liberal Arts tradition and, at the same time, to help young women acquire the ability to make satisfactory adjustment to modern living. Opportunities are presented for the development of all their powers to the end that they may make a vital contribution to the life of their time." Often while in College, students seem carefree and unconcerned, but alumnae reports show, as in 1942, that "practically all lay alumnae are either married or gainfully employed in a wide variety of fields." *Fournier News* in 1940 indicates that all but a few of the fifty-seven seniors have definite plans: graduate school, medical school, business, teaching, and dietetics. Home Economics majors frequently became dietitians in hospitals and, with the coming of the war, in military hospitals. In 1943, six women were engaged in advanced study, three at medical schools. Blanche McIlvaine Kelly, '35, had her own medical practice. There were lawyers, many teachers, and women in a variety of defense positions. War brides emerge, changing the thirties' trend of delayed marriages.

Students were often more aware of world events than was apparent on the surface. The memoirs of a 1944 alumna bear this out: "June 6, 1944—D-Day to all Americans! But to the Class of 1944 it was graduation day from Chestnut Hill College. Rumors had abounded for several weeks thereto that the invasion of Europe was imminent. Our class had spent its entire time at CHC in the war years. Little did we expect on that June morning that we would awaken to the sound of church bells ringing incessantly from as far away as the 'Hill.' Parents, guests, and loving faculty assembled at the appointed hour for the ceremony but needless to say, thoughts were not on the senior girls. There were soft undercurrents of apprehension from all those who had husbands, brothers, and close relatives serving in the European theater. Prayers were being uttered silently and even openly among small groups. . . . Never before or since, can I imagine, the flow of tears that emanated from a CHC graduating class."[38]

As the end of the war approached and victory in Europe seemed more possible, there was a feeling of anticipation in the air. Articles in student publications question the re-election of FDR for a fourth term. He won in the mock elections which again were infallibly on target. The leadership roles played by women in the war led one early feminist to urge greater female participation in social and political spheres. In the final days, alumnae, students, and faculty rose to the national emergency by canceling their events. The sister-students' education, part-time and slow at best, suffered because St. Mary's by-the-Sea at Cape May, the usual retreat site, was used by the U.S. government for military purposes. All retreats were held at Chestnut Hill. Summer classes were greatly reduced, a fact lamented by Sister Maria Kostka who realized the sacrifice this entailed. In 1945, Alumnae Weekend did not take place, and the students' Easter recess was also canceled. This was in compliance with the Office of Defense Transportation. Articles in the *Fournier News* urged everyone to remain, even

students who lived nearby. They did not say how they celebrated the holidays confined to campus, but they are always resourceful.

Chestnut Hill students would later learn the sufferings of those directly involved in the war "when Johnny came marching home again," and from students and faculty from abroad who would come to the College in the post-war years. If some detachment and ivory tower mentality existed among them during the war years, they were probably as involved as any college students, who had never seen war before, and who were concentrating on their education. They were to take their place in society, at home, and as leaders.

Students of the forties learn "modern" equipment

The interior beauty of Residence Hall charmed the first-year students in 1949.
Photo courtesy of Justine Smith Atkins

CHAPTER SIX
POSTWAR YEARS

In May of 1945 the war in Europe ended and in August, the war in the Pacific. As after World War I, an era of prosperity followed. This was a period of complacency, of assurance, lasting through the late forties and into the beginning of the sixties. Styles changed; dresses became more feminine; hemlines were longer in celebration of the abundance of almost everything, including material for clothes. Cars became more available; even some Chestnut Hill students owned them. Finances were better; jobs became less of a concern, and marriage more. The end of the war brought additional young people, and some not so young, to college, many helped by the GI Bill of Rights.

Student publications and administration reports reflect these tendencies. There was an atmosphere of victory, peace, and prosperity. The enrollment was the highest ever, 402, with 146 first-year students. One hundred residents were refused because of lack of space. Residence Hall, a congregational property on Germantown and Sunset Avenues near the College, opened in 1945 with 23 students, under the supervision of Sisters Jane Frances and Francis Xavier. They had a new station wagon and drove up to the College each morning in it, walking up and down the hill during the day. They had all meals except breakfast in the College Dining Room. Some 20 first-year students lived there until Fontbonne opened. In 1963 it became St. Michael's Hall, a residence for sisters.

The College was outgrowing its buildings. Fournier Hall, not adequate for residence, needed more classroom and lab space. The Science Building was erected to continue the work begun by Sisters Eva Maria and Edward Leo in Cincinnati, as the Chestnut Hill Unit of the Institutum Divi Thomae. It was dedicated on May 5, 1947, part of the Centenary Celebration of the Sisters of St. Joseph

Annex residents celebrate Christmas with Sister Eva Maria Lynch in December 1954. Residents reached it by crossing the Arcade, built in 1903 and demolished in 1984, to a floor above the Laundry (now Médaille Center).

The Science Building, a temporary structure in 1947, came tumbling down in March of 1999 to make way for a modern convocation/communications center.

in Philadelphia. Reverend Cornelius Jansen, dean of studies at the Institutum in Cincinnati blessed the building and Dr. Elton S. Cook, dean of research, was guest speaker. While the new building was a welcome, if only temporary, addition to the inadequate science resources, it proved too small. On March 14, 1999, it was demolished, giving way to a bigger and brighter Convocation/Communications Center.

With prosperity came other additions and revivals. Students in *Fournier News* welcomed "more men, cars, cigarettes." Cigarette ads appear in the student newspaper. Seniors claimed the best spots in the "cafe," later "caf," the only place indoors which allowed smoking. Tobacco Road was the outdoor "nicotine lane." No one thought of the dangers of smoking then. Although the College administration did not favor the practice, they thought it was better to designate a safe spot than to risk fires in bedrooms. In 1999, students press for a smoke-free campus.

In scanning student publications at this time the reader notices their very Catholic tone. The 1947 *Aurelian* was dedicated to the one hundred years of the Sisters of St. Joseph in Philadelphia. The 1948 yearbook highlighted the chapel windows in full-page pictures. Editorials in the *Grackle* recommend interpreting literature and life decisions from a Catholic viewpoint. Catholic Press Month (February) always brought a number of editorials in *Fournier News* by prominent Catholic authors, such as on February

13, 1953, Reverend John M. Oesterreicher, noted author; H. C. Gardiner, SJ, literary editor of *America*; and Leo Brady, professor of Drama at Catholic University. Articles and editorials stressed Marian devotion, spiritual preparation for religious feasts, and other devotions. An entire issue of the *Grackle* in 1954 focused on the Marian Year, and the cover was appropriately blue.

Politically, students espoused a strong anticommunist sentiment. Opinions range from outright condemnation to the need for intellectual combat against the "evil." An article in the *Fournier News* in 1948 agrees that Americans should face the Iron Curtain with an iron hand, but disapproves of war. Since most Catholic college students at this time were pro-Franco, another article asks why full UN status should be given to Russia and other communist countries and not to Spain. In 1952 some students attended a symposium sponsored by the Foreign Policy Institute on the possibility of negotiating with Russia. A poll of students and teachers on April 6, 1954, asks about Senator Joseph McCarthy's methods of investigating communists. Opinions are divided; most do not approve of his methods, which others try to reconcile with the American way of life and free speech. Professor William Costello maintains that "the philosophy of communism demands an awake student, an aware student, and above all, an understanding mind."

College women of the forties and

fifties speak about themselves as women, more than in the thirties when they assume that the educated woman graduate would become a leader in society. In 1936 an article in the *Grackle* says that women have become a dangerous contender to the traditional male-dominated society. In the late forties and early fifties, a number of articles stress the growing number of women in science and continued opportunities for them in the military. Career preparation is very important. On the other hand, throughout the fifties, earlier marriages and large families became the trend, and graduates of this period agree that marriage as soon as possible after graduation was expected, since Chestnut Hill and most other women's colleges did not permit married students.

The February 15, 1952 issue of *Fournier News* carries a lengthy discussion of the women's issue. An article had appeared in the January issue of *Mademoiselle* criticizing the college woman for letting the world down. The author, Howard Mumford Jones, finds her losing her intellectual inquiry, apathetic, and indifferent to political issues. "All she wants is a white-collar husband, a ranch type house, and interesting neighbors. She wants children, but will do nothing to make the world a better place for these children to live in." Naturally this spurred a variety of responses from both faculty and students. A male faculty member comments that women are meant to marry, and that professionally women cannot compete with men. Many student responses, though not all, echo similar ideas. They do find women intellectually and politically aware and urge a lowering of the voting age. Yet they see themselves ultimately in the home, and find that their Catholic ideals will see them through. A witty reply to this challenge is found in a few respondents: are male college students any more intellectually alert and politically involved than female?

Articles in the *Grackle* on Kafka, Pasternak, Proust, André Maurois, and Evelyn Waugh suggest keen intellectual

alertness. Students interviewed authors Barry Ulanov and Arnold Lunn. They explored new ideas and produced their own versions of the theater in-the-round and modern art. The designs were creative and in some cases original. Articles in the *Fournier News* continue to emphasize the necessity to vote. In addition to their preoccupation with anticommunism, students explored the Korean conflict and the Anglo-Iranian oil dispute in 1952 when few realized its implications. They heard speakers who kept them knowledgeable about the outside world, such as former professor Eric von Kuehnelt-Leddihn, philosopher Jacques Maritain, and Dorothy Day, founder of the Catholic Worker Movement. They attended meetings with men and women from other colleges. They continued their catechetical work with inner-city youngsters in Philadelphia. They instructed the handicapped at Our Lady of Confidence School. In the summer, they participated in missionary work in the South. Between 1956 and 1962, twenty-five spent a month in North Carolina apostolates. They participated in a forum marking Interracial Justice Week. They conducted a parish census and a house-to-house survey at St. Elizabeth's Parish in the inner city. Not everyone had this level of awareness, but many did. Others came to it later, as alumnae records testify.

There were also direct contacts that brought students and faculty into contact with the world outside Chestnut Hill and indeed outside America. Refugees and exchange students came from Europe and Asia, many telling of their experiences in the war and postwar days. One of the most notable is the historian who was to become famous on both sides of the Atlantic, John Lukacs. He arrived from Hungary and began his career at the College in 1947. Philosopher historian, he looked at everything from Chestnut Hill women to the Cold War and beyond with a critical eye. A simple professor who intrigued his students at first, his name continued to appear everywhere from *Fournier News* to the *New York Times*.

Student refugees came too. *Fournier News* in 1946 tells the story of Simone Lupin from Lyon, France, who took part in the Resistance; Izabella Aldor, born in Poland, who traveled through Europe until she finally reached freedom in Scotland; and Renée Liliana, of French and Russian parentage, who fled through Europe, barely escaping from Lithuania, through Austria, Switzerland, and finally to America. Others came from Germany, Austria, Poland, Ukraine, and other Eastern European nations. Henriette Horschler wrote fondly of her childhood in Austria. Between 1946 and 1950, the College granted full scholarships to ten foreign students: one from Austria, three from China, one from France, three from Germany, and two from Poland. Students and faculty went abroad. Some traveled independently; others joined groups led by Miss Corcoran, Dr. Rita B. O'Mara, and Dr. Lukacs. Fulbright grants brought graduates Gloria Lombardi and Anne McLaughlin to France. The Junior Year Abroad program began in 1956. Paris, Austria, and London were the favorite spots. Amusing accounts in the *Grackle* describe the culture shock of "Americans in Paris." Horizons were expanding.

The faculty too was expanding during these years. Sister Patrick Marie Flood joined Sister Eleanor Marie Miller in the Chemistry Department. Sister Ann Edward Bennis proved a match for

Sister Patrick Marie Flood was chemistry professor and later development director.

Father Lynch in interpreting English literature. John B. Rey brought the flavor of Florence and antique furniture to his French and Italian classes. Josephine Procopio (Albarelli) brought Spanish culture to the fore. Sister Consuelo Maria Aherne gave so many history facts so quickly that dropping a pencil meant missing a century. Sister Marie Thérèse Cogan was "the sound of music" until 1995. William Costello mixed wit and wisdom in his English and Education classes.

Together these people and their predecessors maintained a rich curriculum which, according to the Catalogue of 1950–1951, "provides a balance of required and elective courses, maintaining the integrity of the degree, avoiding too early specialization and preparing the student to make an intelligent choice of a field of study." In 1947, the College became a member of the College Entrance Examination Board, the second Catholic college in the United States to receive this honor. As such, the College could influence academic policy regarding admission of students to higher education. The College was also accepted into the Association of American University Women, giving all graduates the right to membership. A 1956 report indicated that the student body was above average. New students in their first year took the Scholastic Aptitude Test, the American Council on Education Psychological Examination, the Cooperative English Test, and the Iowa Reading Test. No wonder orientation lasted a week.

Curriculum requirements basically did not change. A rather controversial addition was "Natural Science" for non-science majors, a course consisting of Biology, Chemistry, Physics, and Astronomy. The Class of 1958 recalls Sister Grace Marie's Astronomy section: "Despite the fact that our astronomy notes came to us at a speed faster than that of light, and that our ability to take them down was inversely proportional, things could have been worse—Imagine taking astronomy in the year of the sputniks!" Natural Science remained in the curriculum only a few years, since it did not incorporate labs, but it made an indelible imprint on those who took it. Since good ideas are bound to return, Natural Science was reincarnated in 1997, this time with labs.

In 1947, Chemistry was the most popular major; English came next, and History and Social Sciences were third. Articles on women in the sciences abound in student publications; the postwar atmosphere favored science careers. In the sixties and early seventies many of these women returned to the College for updating. Many more graduates went to medical schools. Math major Kathleen McNulty (Mauchly Antonelli), '42, had an unusually spectacular career. She participated in the development of *Eniac*, the ancestor of the modern computer. English majors frequently worked in editing and publishing, from local papers such as the *Germantown Courier* and the *Chestnut Hill Local* to the *New York Herald Tribune*, *The Saturday Evening Post*, and *The American Weekly*. Teaching was popular for all majors.

Physical Education now went from a four-year to a two-year requirement. It included team sports, individual sports, swimming, and dance. Intramurals and varsity sports continued. The fifties were the golden years for swimming. The Aquacade began in 1950 under the direction of Barbara Alexander. At first it was called the Water Ballet, and in 1951–1952 Peggy Watson officially christened it *Aquacade*. Each year had a theme,

Josephine Procopio Albarelli brought Spanish into the fore for almost fifty years.

73

In 1996, to mark the fiftieth anniversary of the computer, "Women in Technology" featured three graduates: Kathleen McNulty Mauchly Antonelli, '42, co-worker on ENIAC; Frances McCullen Pierce, '63, president and CEO of Data Systems Analysts; and Regina Maxwell Schwille, '65, a technical support and management consultant.

such as "The Greatest Show on Earth," "Alice in Disneyland," "Splash of Music." Miss Buckley reports: "The productions grew in scope. Costumes, props, special lights, deck entertainment, an MC—all were gradually added. The swimming numbers became more varied and intricate. New ideas were rife. The pool buzzed with activity."[39] The Aquacade continued for fifteen years, and like many good things, came to an end in 1965.

Faculty-student basketball, softball, volleyball, and badminton games enriched the entertainment. The *Fournier News* of April 23, 1948, reports the basketball game: "A nun's verse choir performed, led by 'proper Bostonian' Miss Gow, in red bloomers and middy . . . at half-time the seniors sat on the floor eating small scraps of oranges, while the faculty sat in regal splendor at a formally set table in the center of the court, eating grapefruit by candlelight. Meanwhile, tall stately Professor of French Mademoiselle

Verspreet amused the students by selling popcorn." Another game in 1956 was equally colorful. The lay faculty players entered in caps and gowns, under which they wore informal sports attire of the twenties. The nuns sang songs; Father Anthony Flynn, professor of Religion, sold popcorn and coke. Who won? The faculty in 1948; the seniors in 1956.

The campus and the city remained the focus of college life. The Glee Club performed at the College and at neighboring men's colleges. Often the event was broadcast on the radio; television was just making its debut. The 1950s were the golden years of the great operas. Students from Chestnut Hill and neighboring men's colleges took all the roles. Louise Burgoyne starred in *Cavalleria Rusticana* and *Faust*; Carol Toscano was later to make her Italian début in *Tosca*; she also appeared with the Philadelphia Orchestra.

The annual Mask and Foil presentation still featured great literary works. Classes presented twenty-minute one-act plays, judged scrupulously by Miss Gow, for the benefit of the missions. The Christmas play *Holy Night* was presented every four years, at Sister Maria Kostka's request, so that each class might have a chance to see it. Students attended these events in large numbers; day students and residents participated; they attended club meetings and lectures, often by force. Involvement was high, although student publications and Student

Council minutes seem to indicate otherwise. By comparison with the sixties, when life began to change dramatically, these were much simpler times.

Yet life was changing at the College. Sister Maria Kostka, who had been at the helm of the College since 1924, was present less and less after 1948. Ill health was weakening this dynamo of energy. Sister Catharine Frances Redmond, dean of students, now gave the Convocation address in September, beginning in 1948, and presided over

Mermaids practice for the Aquacade. *Photo courtesy of the Philadelphia Inquirer*

In a faculty-student basketball game in 1965, the sisters enter the gym singing "When the saints come marching in."

many formal occasions. Students of the early fifties hardly knew Sister Maria Kostka, and she who knew every student in the past did not know them. Finally in 1954, she retired after thirty years as dean and president. Sister Catharine Frances was appointed president, a post which she retained until she too retired in 1968 from ill health. Sister Loyola Maria Coffey remained academic dean, and Sister Gertrude Leonore Lanman came on board as a much-respected dean of students.

Sister Maria Kostka remained on campus as president emerita until shortly before her death when she left for the sisters' retirement home in Cheltenham. There she died peacefully on January 5, 1958. A strong, reticent woman, she has become almost a legend in the annals of the College, and her name remains alive in the Logue Library she so wanted. Her biography is simple; her character much less so. She was born Mary Logue on December 16, 1879, one of four children of Edward and Elizabeth O'Neill Logue. Her father owned a men's cloth-

ing store in Philadelphia, and she grew up at 1526 Callowhill Street. Her childhood was ordinary; she liked pretty clothes and ice-skating. In January, 1898 at age eighteen she entered the Novitiate of the Sisters of St. Joseph. She taught at St. Bridget's, St. Anne's, St. Augustine's, and St. Francis of Assisi before coming to Mount Saint Joseph. She earned her A.B. from Catholic University in 1918 and her M.A. from Villanova in 1923. She received her Ph.D. from the University of Pennsylvania in 1931, while she was guiding the new college through its first steps and teaching History and English. Even today's ACCELERATED and Kirby students can hardly match that for in-service training.

Her thirty years of service at the College show one side of her. But the real Sister Maria Kostka emerges through the many memoirs preserved through the foresight of Sister Grace Margaret Rafferty, archivist from 1983 until her sudden death in 1992. She recorded oral interviews of students and colleagues of Sister Maria Kostka, which paint an excellent picture of the woman who was such an integral part of the College's early history.

Miss Gow's colorful portrait goes back to January 27, 1927, when she first came to Mount Saint Joseph at Sister Maria Kostka's invitation, while in Philadelphia on a lecture tour. She describes a bitterly cold day, and upon arriving at the train station, she thought that she was at the end of civilization. But, she records, "My eyes opened wide . . . when I was ushered into St. Joseph's marble foyer, and the beautiful West Parlor where I waited. Presently a tiny figure entered the room. She looked tiny indeed in that huge room, but I was soon to learn that she was tiny in stature only. In her mind and personality she was a giant, one of the greatest women I have ever known." She asked Miss Gow for a syllabus by March 1. Miss Gow had no intentions of coming, but she prepared the plan anyway, and joined the faculty in 1927. Incidentally, one might give the same description of Miss Gow: tiny in stature only.

Sister Mary Julia Daly's description echoes Miss Gow's. "She was utterly serene. She would walk easily down corridors, always in great serenity . . . Sister Maria Kostka had sparkling brown eyes. She was never hurried. She was, if you will, contained. . . . Even in anger, Sister was never frantic. She never flayed the air about her. She simply smoldered. Sometimes she was livid and cold, but she was always measuring things in a sort of cosmic design. Her hands were very small and always beautifully groomed, and she had a firm, strong, creative and very decorative and distinctive signature. Her voice was strong in inflections and they carried her responses. Her mouth was always controlled. When she smiled, she smiled to one side of her face. That could be a very devastating mark of disapproval at some times. She never engaged in small talk, and she suffered fools badly."[40]

Sister Maria Kostka had to win, in everything from the best possible college to a card game. Many a student remembers Monte Carlo, then the Men's Faculty Room in Fournier Hall, where every night some sisters were drafted for bridge, but did not dare beat Sister Maria Kostka. Once Father Vollmer decided to teach her chess. She obediently followed his directions, until she saw that at every move, he said, "I take." She was enraged; he did not understand the rules of her game. She liked crossword puzzles, and when she did not know a word, she sent for the faculty member in that area, and expected the response quickly. One time she asked Dr. Lukacs for the fifth general in the Confederate line in the Battle of Chatanooga. He knew it at once, and she was very glad that she had hired him.

The Glee Club performs the opera *The Marriage of Figaro* in 1953.

Anne Whiteside (far left) stars as Hecuba in a dramatic rendition of *The Trojan Women* in 1952.

There were two Ellen's in her life. The first was her sister Ellen who opposed her entrance into religion, but later made regular Sunday visits to Chestnut Hill, where the two played cards silently until her sister simply rose and left. The other was her niece Ellen Logue who was a student at the College and a graduate of the Class of 1947. Previously not close to her aunt, Ellen was a bit apprehensive, but fared well with Sister, and made many friends while at the College. She is still a frequent visitor on special occasions and Alumnae reunions, coming from far-off California. Perhaps due to her aunt's influence, she too was a teacher.

With Sister Maria Kostka there was no middle ground; one either liked or disliked her. Many who left their memoirs are the ones who liked, even loved her dearly. Students hailed her interest in them as persons. Freda Gorelick Oben, '40, relates that home concerns were preventing her from finishing her Honors Thesis. She told Sister Maria Kostka who simply said, "Come here, stay here for a few months and be our guest." Freda was of the Jewish faith when she came to college, and became a Catholic because of the influence of such people as Sisters Maria Kostka Logue and Ann Edward Bennis. Freda later became a biographer of Edith Stein, a writer, and translator.

Everyone who speaks of Sister Maria Kostka hails her strength, her infallible sense of excellence in faculty,

Sister Maria Kostka Logue esteemed dean and president, left an enduring legacy at Chestnut Hill College.

a long week in school. She wanted to give them the very best available at the College.

The words of two scholars who knew her well sum up her greatness. Sister Mary Julia says, "Altogether, she was a great mind and a great force. Her College was one of excellence and one of elegance, the flowering of her own excellent mind, her taste, her skill. Chestnut Hill was, indeed, in an Ivy League of its own." And finally John Lukacs who came to America, lonely and alone, and found in Sister Maria Kostka and the other sisters a new family, states: "She was a leader. She had to be a leader. She knew she was a leader."[41]

Sister Grace Margaret Rafferty, as archivist, preserved valuable oral history for the future.

lecturers, and students. She wanted students to be as independent as possible. She appreciated people who gave her an argument. She insisted that *Fournier News* and the *Grackle* be entirely student publications, but she read every word. She also wanted students to take advantage of every educational opportunity, on campus and in the surrounding area. Students in the twenties attended a Greek play at Haverford. Elizabeth Rafferty was encouraged to take the very best English courses with visiting lecturers. Sister Rita Madeleine Gruber recalls that she and a few students were sent into a Medieval History course given by a visiting professor from the University of Pennsylvania. The course just happened to be on Saturday mornings, for the sisters. The students were told to sit up front and ask questions, because the sisters would be tired after

**Sisters Consuelo Maria Aherne and Mary Julia Daly
shared many scholarly projects together.**
Photo courtesy of Sister Florence Edward Sullivan

CHAPTER SEVEN
TRANSITION

The first ten years of Sister Catharine Frances Redmond's administration were peaceful and prosperous. She was a logical successor to Sister Maria Kostka Logue with whom she had worked closely. They shared the same philosophy: train students to independence, give them the best of a liberal arts education, open their minds to the world around them. She encouraged the activities that Sister Maria Kostka fostered for thirty years. She also brought the warmth and gentleness that Sister Maria Kostka often lacked. As Reverend Francis X. McGuire, president emeritus of Villanova, wrote to Sister Mary Xavier Kirby, on September 4, 1968: "I could never find words to eulogize Sister Catharine Frances, your esteemed predecessor. There were few people in our circle of Administrators who moved forward with such calmness, certitude, and vision as she did. It seemed to me always that she was doing the exactly right thing at the exact right time."

One of the first challenges that Sister Catharine Frances faced as president was the Middle States Evaluation of February 7–11, 1956. In preparation, the financial situation of the College needed clarification. As in most other colleges associated with religious congregations, the religious administration managed finances. Middle States now mandated their separation. Everything had to be done in two years. Sister Patrick Marie recalls College committees working together, and departments taking inventory of every piece of equipment they owned. Even bed sheets and pillow cases were counted. The College Business Office opened, near the front door of Fournier Hall, with Sister Jane Frances Duffy as bursar. All was efficiently completed, and the Middle States had high praise for the results. The College was still in the black and morale was high.

The College could have had many more students. Numbers kept increasing, and by 1961 there were 602 full-time students. Space was even more limited. Residents lived all over: in St. Joseph's Hall, in the "Annex," and at Residence Hall. Students who lived within commuting distance would not be accepted for residence. The number

Crowded quarters in the Reading Room of the old Library, St. Joseph's Hall, point to the need of a new one.

of day students, normally about half the population, also increased. They had a life of their own. They gathered at the Loop in Chestnut Hill waiting for the Auch bus that sometimes never came; they met in the "caf," the "day-hop lounge" near the swimming pool, or the DDI (Dew Drop Inn) on the corner of Germantown and Northwestern Avenues. Late permissions and week-ends never touched them, and being less restricted, many held part-time jobs.

A decision about expansion was imperative. The temptation to an extensive building project was very real. Sister Catharine Frances and the Board of Trustees must have instinctively foreseen the changes of the next decade, even the current one.

Participating in the groundbreaking ceremony for the new Library and Residence Hall are Elizabeth Rafferty, alumnae president; Reverend Mother Divine Shepherd Flaherty, chair of the Board of Trustees; Sister Catharine Frances Redmond; and Father Vollmer, chaplain.

They deliberately decided to limit the student body to a maximum of six hundred. This resolution determined the extent of the expansion projects, the selection of students, the size and education of the faculty, and the type of programs in the curriculum. The College decided to remain firm as a small liberal arts college for women,

aiming for what could be done exceptionally well in this role. Since the two most pressing needs were space for residence and library facilities, this was where priorities went.

In her 1958 report, Sister Anne Xavier McGarvey, librarian, gave the reasons for a new Library. Aside from the Middle States recommendation, the space in St. Joseph's Hall was needed for summer and Saturday classes. The weight of the paper was too heavy for the building, and the cost of remodeling would almost equal a new building. She also projected that by 1975, the Library would need five times the current shelf space. Little did she realize that in 1975 similar projections would be made.

Accordingly, the decision was made in 1959 to construct a new Library and Residence Hall, and to move the Academy to the congregational property across Stenton Avenue. Thus St. Joseph's Hall, which housed the Academy, would belong entirely to the College. Sister Catharine Frances at first applied for a federal loan under the Housing and Home Finance Agency, but the regulations were so stringent that the Board decided to finance it by loans and bonds, as it had done with Fournier Hall. The Library and the Residence Hall would be of Mount Airy granite and have red roofs to match the other structures on campus. Dagit Associates were the architects for both buildings; Joseph R. Farrell, Inc., was the general contractor for the Residence Hall, and James J. Clearkin, Inc., for the Library.[42] The entire project, estimated at two million dollars, was entirely repaid by 1974, for the fiftieth anniversary of the College.

Groundbreaking took place on Tuesday, July 19, 1960. After the National Anthem and the Consecration Hymn to St. Joseph, Father Vollmer, College chaplain, blessed the ground. Elizabeth Rafferty represented the alumnae. During the Reunion Weekend of 1958, alumnae had pledged $75,000 within a year. On September 13, 1959, they presented $79,300 in memory of Sister Maria Kostka. Sister Catharine Frances wrote to them, "You are fulfilling what was her most cherished desire in founding the alumnae association: *That the girls would understand their obligations to the College.*"

In 1961 the first class took up residence in Fontbonne. They spoke of it as a "second home for seventy-three

girls, probably away from home for the first time." Beth Schroeder, '65, observed: "When I see an envious upperclassman walking through Fontbonne, I realize how lucky our class is to have the new dorm. What does it matter that the workmen start pounding pipes with sledgehammers below our windows at 8:00 a.m., or that the dust from the Library construction work settles like snow over everything in the rooms, or that there are no curtain rods? Fontbonne is beautiful and it is our home."[43] In 1999, similar noise and dust appear as the new building emerges.

Beautiful indeed it was. Albert J. Dagit, Jr., the architect, described it, "carved from the side of a hill, it has two floors which lead to the grade (and is) designed in the neo-romanesque style." He noted that the exterior windows and doors are of aluminum because it resists corrosion, and the materials were wisely chosen with an eye toward economical maintenance and durability, especially the terrazzo floors and the ceramic tile wainscots, all of which maintain their luster for many years. Students and prefects soon noted that shoes on terrazzo floors well into the night might be practical, but not quiet, so carpets later covered the corridors and a little more peace reigned for those who wanted to sleep or study.

A student's description of Fontbonne Lounge when it received its first visitors on October 22, 1961, Freshman Parents' Day, recalls its original form: "Everyone likes the sleek lines of the Danish modern furniture. Exposed wood blends well with unobtrusive forms; colorful daubs of citron yellow vie with aquamarine splashed to attract the visitor's attention. . . . Pale Nile green chairs are islands of subdued color which offer an interesting contrast to the bold patterns surrounding them." The same chronicler describes the room below it, called the "smoker," and by the summer residents the "peppermint lounge," as "green and white, touched with gold . . . the arrangement of furniture and tiny

83

Fontbonne Hall (right) blends into the architecture of the College.

fringed awnings give the room the casual air of a sidewalk cafe. The reliable soda machine takes second place only to the ash trays which are, after all, the best part of any smoker." These rooms maintained their original decor until the nineties, but the names no longer extol the merits of tobacco.

A feature of Fontbonne was the "tunnel," an underground passage leading to Fournier. Students could get from Fontbonne to the Main Chapel above the Auditorium without ever going outside. Since First Friday Masses and Sodality services were still observed, it was a welcome route to travel. They could also reach class in Fournier and St. Joseph's Hall without risking the elements. On the other hand, on beautiful fall and spring days, some still travel underground and miss some of the finest features of the campus.

The Library required its users to come by way of the outdoors. Would-be book-borrowers might use an underground passage to bypass the front desk. The Library opened in the spring of 1962. In the words of Dagit, "centrally located on campus, the library has its first advantage—it draws students to itself by meeting them along their paths." It had a book capacity of two hundred thousand and a total seating capacity for three hundred. There were four levels of stack area, three seminar rooms, and a language laboratory with individual carrels for forty-two students, used until the technology became obsolete in rapidly changing times. The open stacks were a great boon to researchers who could not have access to many volumes in the space constriction of the old Library.

The most memorable part of the

new Library was how some sixty thousand books got from here to there. Sisters Anne Xavier, Rita Madeleine, and Owen Gertrude conceived the ingenious idea of enlisting students and faculty. Faculty and student officers were monitors; the other students did the actual leg and arm work. On February 5 and 6, 1962, from 9:00 a.m. to 3:30 p.m., students took numbered, colored cards and stacks of books from a teacher in the old Library and carried them to the new one. When they arrived at their destination, they waited until the numbers on the books were called out then put them on the new shelves in exactly the same order as before. There were no classes those two days, perhaps an incentive to complete the project, with accuracy and speed.

Consider, however, what could have happened. An anonymous student

The "Blue Lounge" provided a social atmosphere for Fontbonne, seen here in the early sixties.

writing in *Fournier News*, February 15, 1962, says, "Colleges are masterminds when it comes to military maneuvers.

Life was far from quiet in 1961 as the construction of the Library progressed.

The new Reading Room, bright and spacious, is a contrast to the old one, page 81.

President Kennedy and Arthur Murray consult them before any major move. Unfortunately, students usually manage to turn such perfectly well-thought-out plans into chaos. I have never, never seen anything quite so daring, so well-encompassed as *Operation Book Transfer.* It was magnificently plotted. Naturally our faculty members were worried. How could they even hope to carry out. . . . A plan which included such intricacies as letters and numbers, old stacks and new stacks, east doors and north doors, first floors and second floors? The odds against success were high. . . . Think what might have happened on that first foggy morning if one of the leaders had veered slightly off course—60,000 books in the Wissahickon. Suppose some incendiary-minded history major had hit upon the idea of reenacting the French Revolution. . . . Our reflexes must be slowing down. We did it right. . . . In fact, it should be mentioned on every character reference sheet and every job application that concerns a CHC student. Any girl [who participated] can be counted upon to hold her own under *any* circumstances."

The books were transferred. The new Library, not yet named, was operating. It was not completed yet; in 1961 shelving and equipment were added at the cost of $17,782.00. In 1963 chairs, tables, more shelving, and audiovisual furnishings were installed, at the cost of $84,948.00. Money came from many sources, in addition to the alumnae contributions. In 1962 the W. K. Kellogg Foundation of Battle Creek, Michigan, gave $10,000 to be used over three years in the purchase of books to improve the quality of the College's teacher preparation program, and to increase the effectiveness of its library services. This grant was given to 250 small private, liberal arts colleges, of which seventeen were in Pennsylvania. By this grant, the Foundation wished to recognize the importance of this type of college, which provided 50 percent of teacher education and more than 25 percent of teachers in the United States.

The two buildings were dedicated on St. Joseph's Day, March 19, 1962, at 2:30 p.m. The official ceremony was followed by a reception and tea in St. Joseph's Hall, with members of the faculty as hosts and hostesses. Later, visitors toured the new buildings. Student accounts record a beautiful day with a temperature of fifty-four degrees; adding, "It was a fresh, balmy day, hinting strongly of spring and warm weather. The residents of Fontbonne were enjoying a four-day vacation . . . but the dorm was far from quiet, for visitors—alumnae, ecclesiastical dignitaries and friends—were exploring every nook and corner of Fontbonne." Student Council and class officers, presidents of clubs and associations, editors of publications, conducted tours throughout Fontbonne and the Library after Benediction and the tea. The visitors were impressed by the cleanliness of the buildings, especially the dorm.

Other changes came to the campus decor. St. Joseph's Hall also underwent numerous renovations. In 1964, an automatic elevator helped speed mobility, especially to the improved fifth floor. Here new Physical-Chemistry and Quantitative Analysis labs helped the rapidly expanding number of Science majors. They now had a new Science suite, including a Planetarium, Spectroscopy Room, and Chemistry Lecture Hall. The Planetarium was funded by a grant of $4,010 from the National Science Foundation, and complemented the venerable Observatory. On the ground floor returning students found Histology, Microtechnique, and Microbiology labs. Faculty offices replaced the former Library, and the Alumnae Office moved from its crowded quarters on the first floor of Fournier Hall to a newly expanded area at the site of the former Reading Room. An area with five rooms, forest green carpets and white walls, with lamps of wedgewood green and patterned upholstery, it served as the official quarters of the very active Alumnae Association until 1982, when they moved to Rogers Center.

Students with Sisters Ann Edward Bennis and Mary Julia Daly, left to right, participate in the transfer of books to the new Library.

How the books got from here to there: orderly lines of students!

On the outside, new fire towers conformed to more stringent regulations. The Rotunda, beautiful and awe-inspiring, was also a risk. These towers, built of the same Chestnut Hill stone as the rest of the building, blended in perfectly. They cost $129,800 under a contract from the Frank A. D'Lauro Company. On the third floor the Infirmary was expanded, a new kitchenette added, and a reclining room for day-students installed. The Academy Chapel was tiled in gray and white, gold tapestry backdrops, and gold carpeting on the altar steps. It would again be redecorated in 1978 from the estate of Catherine Benner, '55, and finally cease to function in 1996 due to liturgical changes and space needs.

With finances still in the black, these expenses were not a major concern. Payments could be made regularly to lessen the debt, about $40,000 a year on the principal, and $30,000 on the interest until 1967, when $75,000 to $100,000 was paid on the principal, and $17,000 to $6,000 on the interest. Tuition, room, and board increased gradually. Tuition was $500 in 1954; board $550, and room $100 to $250. In 1964, the combined total was $2,100; day students paid $1,100 in tuition. At the time of the 1956 Middle States evaluation, the salary scale for professors was $4,500 to $6,000; for associates, $3,900 to $5,000; for assistants, $3,300 to $4,300, and for instructors, $2,700 to $3,700. A family bonus of $150 per year was paid for each dependent child under twenty-one years of age. A grant from the Ford Foundation of $164,000 in 1956 was to be held as endowment until July 1, 1966. The income of approximately $7,000 increased lay faculty salaries and furthered the professional advancement of the religious faculty.

After 1966, the money could be used for any educational purpose, but the Board decided to keep it in the Endowment Fund.

Costs were rising and income decreasing. As early as 1961 Sister Catharine Frances began looking for a development director; in 1966 Harold Parks assumed this task. Ominous warnings about the drop in students at private colleges began to appear in the press. Faculty salaries and benefits continued to increase. In 1963, the College agreed to pay the full cost of health insurance for each individual full-time faculty member, Blue Cross and Blue Shield, and Major Medical as administered by TIAA, and to raise its contribution to TIAA from 3.875 percent to 7.5 percent. The family bonus plan was discontinued in 1964. The administration believed that professional salaries should reflect academic achievement, not family size.

Students became more career oriented. Carmela Palermo, '29, returned in 1965 as the director of Placement

John Cardinal Krol, Sister Catharine Frances, Bishop George Leech, and Elizabeth Rafferty head the ceremony of dedication.

89

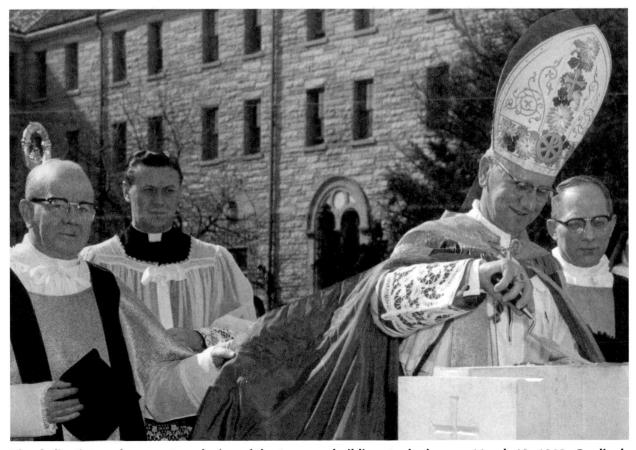

The dedication and cornerstone laying of the two new buildings took place on March 19, 1962. Cardinal Krol officiates.

Louise Bolger, alumnae director, sits in her comfortable new office that was once the Library. It is now made into smaller offices for the business and registrar's personnel.

and Career Guidance. In 1964, *A Profile of Achievement* listed thirty-four medical doctors and nine candidates; 22 Ph.D. Degrees (1938–1964); 91 M.A. Degrees from 1945 to 1954, and 141 from 1955 to 1964, more than half of these from grants. Sisters of St. Joseph graduates of the College obtained 232 additional advanced degrees. Two Fulbright Grants, three Woodrow Wilson Scholarships, two National Defense Scholarships, and one National Science Fellowship were awarded from 1960 to 1964. Science faculty also received many grants. In 1964, Dr. Lukacs was Fulbright visiting professor of History at the University of Toulouse in France, and Sister George Edward (Agnes Josephine Conway) received a scholarship to the American Academy in Rome and the Vergilian Society in Cumae.

Outstanding public distinction in 1964 went to such distinguished alumnae as Kathryn O'Hay Granahan, treasurer of the United States; papal decoration of Pro Ecclesia et Pontifice medal to Dr. Rosalie Reardon, NCCW observer at the World Congress of Lay Apostolate in Rome, and observer for the U.S. Committee of the World Medical Association; Marguerite Farley, named to *Who's Who Among American Women*, assistant director of Radio and TV Programming for the Philadelphia Board of Education; Joanne Malatesta, blind from infancy, supervisor of Philadelphia Nursing Schools for the Blind; Nancy-Joy Gallen Zambelli, fashion coordinator at Bloomingdale's; Kathryn M. Duffy, vice-president of the Invest-in-America National Council; *Fortune* and *Time* circulation manager and executive Marjorie Dyer; diplomatic service agent in many countries in Europe and Asia, Mary Ann Keegan; pathologist (and mother of four children) Dr. Jacqueline Maioriello Mauro; Carol Toscano, winner of the Marian Anderson Award and an opera singer in Europe and the United States. All of these, just a sampling, do not include "the unheralded wives, mothers, and career women, who . . . make of Chestnut Hill a college of distinction." In fact, Chestnut Hill College was listed in *Time* magazine in December 1960 as "one of fifty *Good but little known small*

Sisters (left to right) Regina Dolores Devanney, Marie Thérèse Cogan, and Cecilia Bernard Dougherty congratulate Natalie Nevins for the award she received as a singer in the Lawrence Welk show.

The Motherhouse Chapel, used by the College for formal events, was redone under the direction of Sister Mary Julia Daly in 1954.

colleges in the U.S." It was one of only three Catholic colleges, the other two being Trinity in Washington and St. Mary's in South Bend.

Faculty too attained distinction. Sister Mary Julia participated in the Liturgical Art Exhibit in Philadelphia in 1963. Her work was cited in the *New York Times* as practical and creative. Sister Consuelo Maria, her faithful friend, was invited to teach at Catholic University, and was named advisory editor for the *Catholic Historical Review*. Sisters Eleanor Marie, Patrick Marie, Edward Leo, Miriam Elizabeth, and Paul Daniel continued summer scientific research at far-flung universities, most under grants.

New faculty members came in the late fifties and early sixties. Sister Agnes Josephine Conway, professor of Classics, continued the tradition established by Sister Maria Walburg. Sister Raymond Joseph Murphy enhanced the rapidly expanding Chemistry Department, spending forty-eight years on campus. Sister Helen Veronica McKenna taught Psychology. Sister Mary Xavier Kirby, still exploring Evelyn Underhill at the University of

Pennsylvania, was to become the next president. Other new arrivals were James Sullivan, with an unusual view of history, Walter Zenner, sociologist, and Robert Rowland who trained many teachers. Lester Conner brought the world of Yeats and other Irish and English authors to students, as did Joanna Myers, mainly English. Both saw life in an original way, and were to champion faculty rights. Sister Mary Kieran McElroy also joined the Chemistry Department. On October 1, 1968, she was granted a patent, No. 3403971 for ferri-poly phosphates drying agent, the first faculty member and first Sister of Saint Joseph to gain this distinction. Sister Irma Mercedes (Mary Helen Kashuba, '55) brought Russian to Chestnut Hill in a world still curious and mistrustful of the Russians.

In the early sixties, as in the late fifties, student life did not change dramatically. Student publications show a more questioning attitude among the students; more critical judgment, and greater involvement in the world around them. The curriculum and lectures expanded to nonwestern themes, and in 1962 a yearlong series featured such topics as primitive people and modern Africa, Chinese dance, Islam, and an eastern-rite Mass. In 1966, Rabbi Aaron Landes of the Beth Shalom Congregation conducted a Seder for the entire resident student body. He in turn invited the sisters to his synagogue for Friday evening services. Imagine the consternation of the bus driver when he saw fifty black-garbed nuns filing into a Jewish synagogue!

Students continued to volunteer for service outside the College. In the summer of 1963, eight became members of the Catholic Lay Apostolate in Montgomery, Alabama, and in Pensacola, Florida, and four served as teachers in the Mobile-Birmingham Diocese. A student served as a delegate at a White House Conference, only one of five from Catholic women's colleges. In the same year, the Catechetical Group received an honorary citation for twenty-five years of uninterrupted ser-

91

Alumnae leaders enjoy the great day: President Nancy Peck Perkins, Vice-President Jane de Paschalis Kane, Chairman Barbara Beers Oberle, Publicity Chairman Mary Walker, and Area Chairman Barbara Carli, of Vineland, N.J.

Left to right: Mr. Wallace Magill chats with Chairman Barbara Beers Oberle '55. Gary Karr in the background.

Left to right: Mrs. George Porreca, Parents' Committee Chairman, Joanne Waldron Dwyer '55, Ticket Chairman, Nancy Peck Perkins '43, Alumnae President, Francis Heilbut, accompanist, and Mimi Givnish Quinn '52, Philadelphia Area Chairman, discuss the concert.

Lincoln Center

May first dawned brilliantly clear, and Lincoln Center Day was perfect from beginning to end. Almost 2600 Chestnut Hill alumnae and their friends enjoyed the benefit concert at Philharmonic Hall, and visited with friends and college faculty at the pleasant reception later. Barbara Beers Oberle '55, dynamic chairman of the history-making affair, has not yet announced final results, but she rejoiced with everyone over the day's spectacular success. The concert included premiere performances of two compositions.

Sister Catharine Frances meets Gary Karr, concert artist.

Concert performers Jeffrey Siegel, Mary Burgess, Gary Karr meet Sister Catharine Frances, Chairman Barbara Beers Oberle and Sister Loyola Maria. Accompanist Francis Heilbut completes the group.

Alumnae Vice President Marguerite Farley and Publicity Chairman Mary Walker visit with Sister Maria Walburg.

Alumnae, faculty, and friends attend a concert at Lincoln Center to celebrate the fortieth anniversary of the College in 1964.

vice. In the summer of 1964, six students participated in "Operation Discovery," to aid and encourage culturally deprived children to further their educations. Students went to Pennhurst State Hospital to teach prayer and catechism to the mentally challenged. Others went to Casa del Carmen to interact with the growing Hispanic population of Philadelphia. Students also tutored at Carson Valley School, and took door-to-door census in an inner-city parish. Many reported "a feeling of warmth and satisfaction that they are doing something worthwhile with their free time."

And yes, there was still the fun. Dances, plays, concerts, continued to fill the College woman's day. Sports, both on and off campus, were important. Witness the witty articles by Rosemary Scheirer '58 (now SSJ): *Schei Spies.* New varsity sports such as lacrosse replaced softball in 1960. The archery team, in existence since 1939 with some interruptions, had four undefeated years from 1952 to 1956. Basketball teams remained undefeated from 1963 to 1965. Varsity golf, with many winners in the late fifties, did not survive the sixties. A. A. Days, Doggie Roasts, Bermuda Shorts Parties added fun to the competition. Some began to see their demise in the sixties.

The year 1964 was the fortieth anniversary of the College. A special celebration was held on May 1, 1965, at Philharmonic Hall in Lincoln Center. Almost twenty-six hundred alumnae and their friends attended, with many of the faculty joining them. The benefit concert for Chestnut Hill, chaired by Barbara Beers Oberle, '55, featured premiere performances of two compositions. It was a bright beautiful day, closing a year that featured concerts and lecturers, including Moira Walsh, noted film critic for *America*. She was the daughter of James Walsh who was on the original faculty, and in whose memory the Walsh Medal for philosophy was given. Students delved into the past, and found interesting anecdotes which they faithfully recorded in their publications.

Yet a different future was emerging. In a fortieth anniversary editorial for *Fournier News*, October 26, 1964, Sister Catharine Frances Redmond wrote: "One of the most obvious changes we observe during these decades here is in you, the student. Born during and after World War II, your interests are away from the campus to the world about you. You are involved, but in a different way from the girl of the twenties, the thirties, and the forties. In this era of a *new Pentecost* and *new moonshots*, you represent a new confidence, a new independence; in short, a *New Breed*." Wisely she recognized it, but it would not be she who would deal with the radical changes that were just around the corner. Yet before we explore the changes, let us see what remained and remains to this day: tradition!

93

Margaret Healy Haney poses as May Queen in 1933. *Photo courtesy of Margaret Haney*

How many times do students say, "We have begun a tradition." They speak of the first annual dance or show or play. Sometimes it is the last annual one as well, as the first class speaks of their freshman prom: "thoroughly unbusinesslike and quite enjoyable—this was unfortunately not repeated." Yet many customs did remain: May Day, Halloween Party, Student Government, Family Weekend, Investiture with cap and gown, A.A. Day, hazing of first year students, big sisters and stepsisters, the annual retreat, junior and senior proms and, most of all, Christmas celebrations.

May Day started with a gambol on the lawn in 1925. In 1929 under Miss Elizabeth Somers Ford it took on an elaborate form. Dorothy Barton describes the first events, which took place outdoors where the Library is now situated. It was "based on the English May Days with May Queens, daisy chains, games and dances. Daisies grew profusely in the fields where the present Academy is located. Miss Gow would contribute by directing scenes from *A Midsummer Night's Dream* or *Robin Hood*. I laugh when I remember changing costumes from the Queen's Court, to Titania, to the top of an acrobatic pyramid. . . . [Another] was a Greek Pageant based on *The Legend of the Laurel*. It was held on the beautiful expanse of lawn in front of the Summer House. It was all in dance and pantomime with a background of broad white steps and Grecian pillars. Sister Maria Walburg prepared a group to speak the Odes in Greek. Sister Maria Kostka went with me to the Allen's Lane Theatre, where I was a member, to inspect the pillars before I gained permission to borrow them."[44]

Historically, May Day was a Roman celebration from April 28 to May 2 in honor of Flora, the goddess of flowers. May Day in medieval and Tudor England was celebrated by young and old. Villages vied with one another for

MT. ST. JOSEPH COLLEGE

presents

The Queen's Festival

Oh hear ye, citizens of this domain,
 The lovely Queen of May
Together with her beauteous train,
 Comes here to visit us today.
A festival we'll order in her name
 With dances and a play,
We'll strive to win her royal acclaim
 In our poor country way.

With her are lovely, waiting-ladies four
 And all the brilliant court,
Her dancers bring their well-learned lore
 While we are just—self-taught.
But dance we shall in our own way
 And act with might and main,
We are the subjects of the Queen of May,
 We'll strive to win her loved acclaim
 In our poor country way.

COLLEGE CAMPUS

MAY 29, 1934   4 P. M.

PROGRAM FOR MAY DAY

PROCESSIONAL

Queen . . . . *Regina Motzenbecker*
Court . . . . . . *Cora I. Donnelly, Madge G. Gannon, Florence M. Sandberg, Edna M. Sieck*
Pages . . . . *Gertrude Crumbie, Rita Pfluger*
Queen Crowned by . . . . *Evelyn E. McCloskey*
(Student Council President)

Student Body

CROWNING OF THE QUEEN . . . . *Evelyn E. McCloskey*
ENGLISH FOLK DANCE—"Sweet Kate" . . . . *Freshmen*
MAYPOLE DANCE—Sellinger's Round . . . . *Freshmen*
IRISH FOLK DANCE . . . . *Freshmen*

SPREADING THE NEWS
By LADY GREGORY

BARTLEY FALLON . . . . *Bettina Clemons*
MRS. FALLON . . . . *Kathleen Holmes*
JACK SMITH . . . . *Betty Ann Troy*
SHAWN EARLY . . . . *Ruth Mack*
TIM CASEY . . . . *Veronica McClane*
JAMES RYAN . . . . *Josephine Cotter*
MRS. TARPEY . . . . *Betty McHugh*
MRS. TULLY . . . . *Roseanne Cusack*
JO MULDOON . . . . *Jeanne Smith*
MAGISTRATE . . . . *Mary McQuillan*
TOWNSPEOPLE: *Zelphie Cohalan, Elsie Kokes, Mary Napier, Elizabeth O'Hanlon, Dolores Golden, Harriet Fitch, Claire Crumbie, Rita Whalen.*

SCENE: The outskirts of a Fair—an Apple Stall.

MODERN DANCE GROUP

FOLK THEME . . . . *Sophomores*
THREE INTERPRETATIONS OF A DUTCH DANCE COMPOSED IN
 CLASS . . . . *Sophomores*
 (1) Pursuit.   (2) Invocation.   (3) Caprice.
HARVEST RITUALS . . . . *Sophomores*
REVELS . . . . *Juniors*
RHAPSODIE . . . . *Sophomores*
ECOSSAIS . . . . *Sophomores*
RECESSIONAL

This program announces the May Festival in 1934.

The class of 1948 dances around the Maypole.

the height and decoration of their Maypole. Young people danced around it, weaving colorful patterns with ribbons. Cromwell outlawed the Maypole as too frivolous, and the Puritans never allowed it in America. May Day, however, was reincarnated on many college campuses, with celebrations not unlike Chestnut Hill's.

The College Festival was called: *May Festival, The Queen's Festival, May Fair,* and finally *May Day*. In 1932, the Queen was attended by six seniors in her court in Elizabethan costumes, a page, and a jester. Dancers wore village costumes. The Glee Club sang "Kerry Dance" and "Piper June." The Mask and Foil presented Shakespeare's *Pyramus and Thisbe*. The identity of the May Queen was kept secret until she appeared with her attendants, but by 1933 it was announced two weeks earlier in *Fournier News*.

The Festival took place at 4:00 p.m. on the campus. In 1933 there was an elaborate procession around the

College. Two floats, colorfully decorated and drawn by horses, carried the cast of the play and the Queen and her Court. In 1936 printed programs contained the names of patrons, and announced an effort to inaugurate an Endowment Fund. The students raised $1,000, a handsome sum for the Depression. They presented a Fashion Show, sponsored by Oppenheim Collins and Company of Philadelphia, an Art Exhibit of students' work, and social dancing in the "Summer Pavillion," with music by the Villanovans. In 1939, songs and dances came from Scotland, Ireland, and America. The Verse Speaking Choir performed. In 1940 a Greek play dramatized a musical competition between Apollo and Pan. Students wore pastel Grecian gowns, representing flower maidens, sun nymphs, handmaidens, and bacchanal dancers.

The day began and at first also ended with a religious celebration. After morning High Mass in the Convent Chapel the prefect of the

For the May Day celebration of 1949 students gather in the Convent Chapel with Sister St. Luke Kelly's paintings, before the renovation.

Sodality crowned Mary. A procession and second crowning by the Student Government president took place at the Grotto. Since only resident students attended this liturgy, May Day has always come to mean the gambol on the lawn. The thirties were its golden years, with elaborate plays, music, dance, and costumes. The account and plans occupied a prominent place on the first page of *Fournier News*, with a picture of the May Queen.

The year 1941 brought a change in the program. The event, hereafter on the last Sunday in May, was totally in the hands of the students. A new tradition began: the students made their own skirts, leading to the frantic last-minute pinning and stapling. The classes composed songs to Stephen Foster melodies and the applause of the audience decided the winner. In 1942 simplicity was the style, in keeping with the war. During the patriotic war years, classes chose American themes.

The postwar period did not revive the earlier elaborate festivities, but it saw the entire senior class in formal dress seated on risers and entertained by the other classes. Themes featured the four seasons, continents, the phases of college life and for the last May Day in 1959, "Let there be music." The pattern remained the same: juniors greeted the seniors with a daisy chain; sophomores danced around the Maypole. There was a song competition; seniors chose the winning class.

As time went on, the coverage in *Fournier News* decreased; on two occasions, even relegated to page two. The May Queen's picture no longer appeared. The same themes recurred; fewer and fewer skirts saw a needle and thread. When May Day was discontinued after 1959, there was hardly a comment in the student publications. Yet as the importance of May Day waned, Christmas took on all the elaborate trappings formerly reserved for the legendary spring festival.

Christmas at Chestnut Hill is an uninterrupted, living tradition. In 1924, the first class, after "singing vociferously if not melodiously the night before Christmas vacation," surreptitiously entered the sisters' Community Room and decorated a tree for them, with a present for each sister. Alas, when they arrived the next morning to see the results of their work, the tree had fallen down. Undaunted, they tried again; this time it stayed up. The Class of '28 remained in charge of the decorations for four years, giving the caroling to sophomores, their privilege until the more general Carol Nights in the 1980s.

The seniors considered the decorations their gift to the administration and faculty, especially the sisters, who all resided at the College. When

Fournier Hall opened, a tree graced the foyer outside the Dining Room, and faculty received gifts. The sophomores, attired in cap and gown and carrying lighted candles, made their way through the darkened corridors from the Rotunda along all the corridors of Fournier, singing carols and leaving candy at each door. Later they marched outdoors. With the arrival of Miss Gow came a religious Christmas play. The Athletic Association sponsored parties, and Sister Hilarion provided refreshments for everyone. The Home Economics students served the famous "charter cookies," so named in 1927 when the department sought and received certification, supposedly because of the cookies.

The decorations, still the prerogative of the senior class, grew and developed, with a second tree in the Main Foyer of the College. Students decked offices and teachers' rooms, tables in the Dining Room and the Cafeteria. The decorations soon spilled out into the corridors, with fresh greens, holly, and bells. In 1943, the seniors created an outdoor scene with banks of imaginary snow and a large white angel. The main foyer was more religious in nature; other areas had a secular theme. There was a color theme until the late forties. The plans, not secret until the sixties, were publicized earlier in the *Fournier News*.

Refreshments after carols quickly grew into the Candlelight Tea, prepared by the sophomores. It was held at 6:00 p.m., both in the Dining Room for residents and the Caf for day students. The sophomores decorated the tables rather ingeniously, keeping their theme a secret until the event. They chose caroling snowmen, angels, miniature sleighs, and candles. Santa Claus distributed presents to the seniors, prepared by the sophomores for their big sisters. Seniors received a rose or a Christmas corsage. Clubs and associations and especially seniors held parties and special Christmas events. Beginning in 1955, lay faculty and their spouses were invited to the Christmas dinner, previously held for

Juniors carry the traditional daisy chain for the May Queen.

The May Queen is crowned by the president of the Student Council in the early 1940s.

residents only.

In 1950 and 1957 the seniors chose a medieval theme. They transformed the main foyer into a cathedral, modeled after Chartres, with two rose windows. Angels inspired by Fra Angelico adorned the chapel doors. Garlands in the Della Robbia style graced the corridor, while the area outside the Dining Room featured prophecies about the coming of Christ. Even the Glee Club chose medieval carols. Religious themes predominated in the fifties, a decade with strong Catholic overtones. Father Vollmer blessed the tree, and the festivities ended with a visit to the chapel.

The sixties brought more secular themes. The Class of 1963 featured Japanese culture in keeping with the Oriental Lecture series. They used figures with black and gold lines against a flame background with chrysanthemums, and trimmed the tree in gold with candle lights to represent the Japanese "tree of light." Later seniors chose "Babes in Toyland," a "Dickens Christmas," and an "Old Fashioned Christmas." The Class of 1966 depicted the Renaissance, to honor the seven hundredth anniversary of Dante's birth. By 1965, the Dorian Club joined in the Christmas festival, and the German Club gave its annual Weinachtspiel.

The Christmas Dinner, gradually replacing the Candlelight Tea, culminated in a surprise dessert prepared by Sister Francis Xavier. For many years sparklers flickered off rounded lazy susans, carried by the sophomores. Students dressed in their best attire, and, for only this once, were allowed to smoke in the Dining Room. In 1966, the junior class began to sponsor a Christmas dance in the gym, open to all, and served refreshments in the decorated Lounge. The dance later moved to the Rotunda, which the juniors decorated in elegant fashion, their annual prerogative.

Everything changed in 1968, as did Christmas. The Mask and Foil presented an integrated ballet representing

Bishop Fulton Sheen was a frequent visitor at Chestnut Hill's May Days. Here he is seen with his secretary, Edythe Brownette, a former May Queen and Sister Mary Magdalen Yauch, both '48.

Sophomores in the forties prepare the Candlelight Tea.

the Black-White Confrontation in America. The Glee Club, now under the direction of Carl Suppa, presented an evening concert, featuring the debut of the College Chorale. In 1969–1970, students were involved in peace movements and in protests against the War in Vietnam. On October 15, 1969, many signed a "Plan for Peace" under the guidance of French Professor Anne Callahan; therefore the only sign of Christmas was the tree in the Foyer and the Christmas Dinner.

Life however returns to normal, and the traditional Christmas reappeared. "Babes in Toyland," "White Christmas," and the unforgettable "Camelot" graced the corridors. With the retirement of

Miss Gow, the Christmas plays ended, as did the German play with the demise of clubs. Decorations became more and more elaborate, sometimes almost blocking the corridor. Mannequins appeared, dressed in imaginative costumes. In 1978, the whole Cratchett family sat around a table outside the Dining Room, and Marley's ghost emerged from a dark corner of nineteenth-century English shops. The theme was kept a deep secret, and there was little faculty involvement. All classes worked far into the night, and often were not finished by daybreak. Anxious to see the reactions of the younger students, seniors played music over the public address system to awaken the sleepers.

Less elaborate because of fire regulations, the decorations after 1983 often took on an elegant simplicity reminiscent of the early days. "Christmas around the World," presented by the Class of 1988, featured a live outdoor Nativity scene, with readings and prayers in various languages. The Christmas Dinner became the Senior Dinner. Santa Claus, otherwise known as Father Casey, beloved by all the students of the eighties, and a tradition in his own right, appeared during the dinner. Young and old, especially children, flocked to the carols in the Rotunda and another visit from Santa.

The decade of the nineties has brought deeper meaning to Christmas, since the senior classes donated some of the money they raised to a local

Sophomores gather around the Christmas tree in 1947 for the traditional carols.

charity. Christmas has brought much to Chestnut Hill, and Chestnut Hill much to Christmas. Students work together, especially seniors. They learn cooperation and respect for others' ideas. They learn to plan early, some-

This Nativity scene from Oberammergau, a gift of Sister Rita Madeleine Gruber, had a central place in the Christmas decorations.

Ceramic Christmas trees decorate the tables in the sixties as surprised seniors enter.

times deciding on a theme as juniors. The masterpieces are photographed far and wide, and appear in local newspapers and on television. Students' families and friends and hundreds of people from the neighborhood drop by

every year before, during, and after the season. It is a tradition to remember.

A less formal tradition is Halloween. The early classes tell about a ghost walk in the cemetery after lights out, only to find the lights on in the sisters' rooms, and they were caught. Students also donned costumes which were judged for originality. During the Depression all were invited to come in costume, with no admission charge because of the difficult economic times. From the forties to the sixties, Halloween was the prerogative of the sophomores, who made up skits and songs. Costumes and parties still remain, along with competitions in room and hall decorations. Resident assistants leave a treat at each one's door and the fun goes on.

On a more solemn note, academic Investiture created a scholarly atmosphere. In the twenties and thirties, first-year students received their caps and gowns on or around October 15, known as Founders' Day from the foundation of the Sisters of St. Joseph in 1650. Sister Mary Julia tells how the students "would line in a choral sort of group, maybe ten abreast, and would advance up to the Social Room toward the line of throned chairs on which sat . . . the Council of the Community. Sister Maria Kostka would present each girl by name and the particular parish or city from which she came. Reverend Mother would speak personally to her . . . and was often acquainted with their professional fathers. . . . The girls at that time would receive their caps and gowns, and as they left Reverend Mother, they would move to the back row so that when

The surprise dessert and sparklers are borne into the Dining Room by sophomores.

they advanced again, all were dressed in cap and gown, all having been singularly honored at that particular ceremony."

Academic dress was worn at formal college gatherings, such as Sodality meetings, First Friday Masses, Honors Convocations and, in the thirties, for Christmas carols, indoor and outdoor. In the 1950s, Investiture occurred in the spring of sophomore year, during the Honors Convocation. Only juniors and seniors wore the cap and gown; underclass members were required to dress appropriately, with dresses or blazers and heels. With the revolts of the early seventies, Investiture disappeared, and academic dress was worn only at Graduation. The nineties saw a return of the Investiture ceremony at a special liturgy during Family Weekend, in the fall of senior year.

Sister Catharine Frances began Family Day to raise money and to involve students' families more with the College. The first chairman was Mr. William Whiteside, father of Anne and Sperky. Parents came on Friday afternoon, attended classes with their daughters, met with the faculty, and had an informal buffet supper. In the evening, Fashion Design majors modeled their own creations in the Auditorium. The day ended with a father-daughter dance, and a card-party for the mothers. Four hundred people attended the first Family Day on May 11, 1956.

This pattern, with some variations, continued until the changes of the late sixties. Faculty members lectured. The Fashion Show became more and more elaborate, under the direction of Sister Stella Bernard Gardner, until the Fashion Design major was discontinued in 1971. The shows had a theme; in 1961, "The Lithe Look in Our Nation's capital," with a backdrop of the Washington Monument and cherry blossoms. The Card Party held on the first Family Day was moved to another time, and used

The Class of 1988 presented a live Nativity scene outdoors, accompanied by prayers and songs in many languages.

as a fund-raiser.

As the waters calmed in mid-seventies, Family Day became Parents' Weekend, ending with an elaborate liturgy in the

The Chestnut Hill Plan for Peace

How can we be most effective in bringing about an end to American participation in the war in Vietnam? Let the government and the people know of our displeasure through a non-violent yet a forceful way. We at Chestnut Hill can abandon a quiescent, by-stander's role and become leaders in the Protest for Peace, and we can do this by submitting our plan to the community. The Chestnut Hill Plan for Peace is very simple and can be simply stated. Postpone Christmas.

The Feast of Peace will come only when Peace comes to Vietnam!

If, until our goal is reached, we can convince a sufficient number of our fellow citizens not to buy a tree, an ornament, a gift, a piece of wrapping paper or a card, it will focus upon the American will for Peace more effectively than anything stated and advanced until now.

What greater tribute to the meaning of Christmas can we pay? Let's put an end to hypocrisy. Do we mock Christ, the Prince of Peace, if we celebrate on the one hand, in our usual lavish way, while on the other hand this terrible war is waged by our people? Can we lead the way to a celebration of his birth that will be honest and meaningful, that will at last be Christian. Can we demonstrate to the community the possibilities of Peace on Earth, good Will Toward Men.

Such a dedication will mean sacrifice. There should be no strings of many-colored lights, no presents to open this year. This year Christmas should be a time of recollection, not our affluence. We must demonstrate this not only to others but to ourselves, within our families, a proof, through sacrifice, that we have the personal courage of our public convictions.

What an opportunity for us. ARE WE SINCERE enough to do this? Are we honest enough? AND WE CHRISTIAN ENOUGH?

I, _____, pledge to support the Chestnut Hill Plan for Peace.   October 15, 1969

The "Plan for Peace" calls for a moratorium on the celebration of Christmas in 1969.

Preparations for Christmas decorations in 1984, as in most years, last far into the night.

Mannequins bring Christmas alive during the early 1980s.

Main Chapel. It still included events from the past, such as the dance, lectures, and the faculty-family tea. The date was moved to October, and often took on the overtones of an Oktoberfest. Saturday was the fun day; Sunday the more formal event. Saturday brought such events as a Carnival, sports events, and a Casino (often run by the sisters). In a more inclusive term, the weekend became Family Weekend. Students of the eighties and nineties selected themes: "Mardi Gras" in 1988, "A Visit to the Medieval Kingdom" in September of 1992, and "The Roaring Twenties" in 1993. Family Weekend continues to feature newer activities, including a Homecoming for alumnae, and a Fall Festival. It is an event that students, family, and friends can enjoy together.

A more recent tradition, Gourmet Day, is tied to the student foreign language newspaper, *Kosmos*. Begun by Denise Wade, '78, *Kosmos* first appeared in 1977, and published articles in languages studied or spoken on campus. It won a first place award in 1985 and 1988, and second place in 1991, from the American Scholastic Press Association, and continued publication until 1991. Gourmet Day started in 1978 to support *Kosmos*. Students cook or solicit ethnic foods, and sell them at reasonable prices. Members of the College community and friends buy the delicacies or take them home for the night's supper. Local

Father John Casey was everything from Santa Claus to a compassionate grandfather figure to students in the eighties.

Ring Day was a special celebration for the junior class. Shown here are members of the class of 1953 at their Ring Day Luncheon in 1952. *Photo courtesy of Justine Smith Atkins*

Family Day, begun by Sister Catharine Frances Redmond, became an important annual event. She is seen here (left to right) with Mrs. George Porreca and Mrs. Stanley Duckworth, co-chairs, and Mr. Henry Schmidt, vice-president.

Rebecca Williamson and Ruth Anne Flynn model "1958 Styles in Old Philadelphia" for the Fashion Show for Family Day.

restaurants and stores donate food items or gift certificates. If *Kosmos* has slumbered, Gourmet Day remains alive and well. Campus and neighborhood look forward to the event.

These are among the most memorable traditions for all members of the College community. They have helped to bring students together, to give them a sense of responsibility, and to bring the College into the view of the broader community. Hopefully they will remain for many more years and give everyone a chance to say "Remember when?"

 Students and friends provide entertainment as well as food for Gourmet Day.

KÓSMOS

The ROMAN EMPIRE
at its greatest extent
117 A.D.

Mediterranean Sea

ARABIA

MUNUS EX MARI
PROOEMIUM.

by
Anne Morrow Lindbergh

Translated by
Karen Quinn

Litus non est locus
ubi bene laboratur, aut
legitur, aut cogitatur.
Haec a prioribus annis
meminisse debui. Tam
calidum, tam umidum,
tam lene est ut nec
meam mentem exercere
nec de rebus altis cog-
itare possim.

Numquam discitur.
Id saccum stramineum,
crassum propter libros,
schedam puram, epistu-
las diu debitas, stilos
nuper acutos, tabulas,
et consilia bonaomnia
ad litus magna cum spe
feruntur. Libri sunt
not lecti, stili frag-
unter, schedae sunt
blandae et integrae

plaudenteshi omnes
sonos urbis et suburbii
temporis et spatii fe-
briculosos, obscurant.
Incantata, te relaxas,
te pronan extendis.

Velut elementam in quo
iaces, aequa mari fis;
nuda, aperta, cassa
sicut litus de quo
omnes adumbrationes
hesternas aestibus hod-
iernis delentur.

Tum denique, non-
nullis post diebus,
aliquo mane animus ipse
exoitatus de novo vivi-
sset - non urbane, min-
ime, sed in rhythmo
littoris.

Fluitare, ludere,
sequitur et placide
volvere incipit, sicut
undae segnes quae in
litus sequitur volvunt.
Quas divitias fortuitas
haec fluctus placidae
in blandam arenam albam
animi iactent, numquam
scis...

Sed non expetendum
est aut - prohibeat

CONNAISSEZ-VOUS
LE LIBAN?

Jadis, on l'appelait
'La Suisse du Moyen-
Orient'. Sa location
géographique, liant
l'Europe à l'Asie,
l'avait transformé à
un centre commercial
et banquaire. Beirut,
la capitale, était
l'endroit où se rencon-
traient les hommes
d'affaires Arabes et
Occidentaux. Chaque
année, des milliers de
touristes passaient
au Liban pour jouir de

by Nada Khalife

ans. En vue du pro-
blème Palestino-
Israelien, plusieurs
centaines de refugiés
Palestiniens se sont
établis sur ce terri-
toire, titubant la bal-
ance confessionelle.
Cette nouvelle situa-
tion a ouvert la porte
des désaccords politi-
ques, sociaux et écono-
miques. Le 13 Avril
1975, la guerre civile
a éclaté.
Durant 20 mois, une

The masthead of *Kosmos,* taken from the first issue in 1977, reveals its international character.

Sister Clare Joseph O'Halloran is a legend at the College as longtime registrar and directress of the A.B. candidates among the Sisters of Saint Joseph. She is pictured here at her famous Bulletin Board.

CHAPTER NINE
CHALLENGE

The students of the sixties were indeed "a new breed," as Sister Catharine Frances Redmond observed. Vatican II had swept over the Catholic Church, bringing winds of change. The liturgy was no longer in Latin; new hymns and new forms of worship appeared. Religious life would be altered dramatically; Catholic schools closed as fewer people entered religion and others left. Vatican II urged a return to earlier, simpler observances and placed the emphasis on the laity. The results were greater personal responsibility and more questions.

Throughout the world people were questioning, especially the young. When the United States entered the Vietnam War in 1962, no burst of patriotism inflamed the country, as in the two world wars. People protested against the war and burned draft cards. Some did serve in the military, and if they returned they faced indifference, even derision. The war dragged on until 1973, and hung like a cloud over the nation and the world. On the brighter side, people sailed into space, beginning in 1962, and walked on the moon in 1968. Possibilities seemed limitless.

The Kennedy years brought a feeling of Camelot to the country, shortened by the assassination of President John F. Kennedy in 1963. Later assassinations of Robert F. Kennedy and Martin Luther King Jr. in 1968 profoundly affected morale. King preached a peaceful solution to segregation; his untimely death saw the movement sometimes turn to violence in urban riots. Anger and rebellion were in the

Miss Gow and Father Lynch followed by Betty Buckley and Josephine Albarelli march in the Academic Procession for Graduation ceremonies held in the Dining Room until the late sixties.

air, as was a new sense of freedom.

It was from this world that young women came to Chestnut Hill in the sixties. They came from traditional, mostly Catholic, and conservative families. They came to a college that was equally traditional, Catholic, and conservative. Slightly extended permissions still remained strict. Students wore skirts at all times except for sports, and even then a coat was required in the halls and on the campus. A sister lived on every corridor in the residence halls. She checked each room at 10:00 p.m. and offered the students holy water (along with a bit of conversation and friendly advice more often than not). Three-day retreats were of obligation, silence expected, and formal conferences held. Men were strictly excluded from dorm rooms. Failure to respect the sign-out book was a capital offense.

This situation was typical of many women's colleges in the country, but another factor influenced Chestnut Hill College. Faculty and administration stayed for many decades. Retirement was unknown in any religious community unless health made it imperative. The early lay faculty also stayed. Thus the vibrant teachers of the twenties and thirties were still active in the sixties. Although younger ones had come, it was the veterans who made policy. President Sister Catharine Frances began to suffer from failing health. Miss Corcoran ably and quietly kept the ship afloat during the last years of Sister's administration. Although Sister recognized the new breed of student, she was unable to assess the magnitude of the situation.

The year 1968 was crucial. Student riots in Europe spread to the United States. Chestnut Hill students became

111

more restless. They began to question not only their regulated social life, but also the curriculum. Distributional requirements had hardly changed since the 1930s; students wanted more options and more practical courses. Department chairs never rotated. The student government role reverted to supervising nonfunctioning clubs and student offenders. Students wanted a share in decisions that would affect them.

The year 1968 brought shared decision-making to the Sisters of St. Joseph in a unique General Chapter that elected delegates from among the "rank and file." It also brought a new administration to the congregation, among them historian Sister Consuelo Maria Aherne. With their encouragement, Sister Catharine Frances resigned in 1968. A member of the College faculty since 1930, dean of students in 1939, and president in 1954, she had given thirty-eight years of service to Chestnut Hill. Her ill health soon brought her to St. Joseph's Villa.

Meanwhile the task of leader fell to Sister Mary Xavier Kirby, a relative newcomer to the College, having arrived in 1959. She was not a graduate of Chestnut Hill, but rather of New Rochelle in New York. A member of the English Department, a talented writer herself, she had just completed her Ph.D. at the University of Pennsylvania with a dissertation on the Anglican mystic Evelyn Underhill. Since she spent her years at the College studying and writing, she did not absorb the fullness of tradition, and thus was at an advantage in handling change. Like Sister Maria Kostka, she was new to the challenge of leading a college. She had been a popular teacher. Wit and wisdom, and her interaction with people gave her success.

Change immediately faced Sister Mary Xavier. In 1968 Sister William Marguerite (Margaret Fleming, '56) became dean of students. In 1969, Sister Helen Veronica McKenna became academic dean, and in the following year Sister Grace Margaret Rafferty, registrar. Sister Theresa Connor pre-

Sister Mary Xavier Kirby is named the fourth president of the College in 1968. She is seen here with her successor, Sister Matthew Anita MacDonald, at the dedication of her portrait.

pared to succeed Sister Jane Frances in 1973. This same team worked well together throughout Sister Mary Xavier's tenure, 1968–1980. Sister lists this as one of her greatest assets.

The years 1969 to 1972 saw many retirements. Among them: Sister Clare Joseph (1925–1970), registrar and director of Sisters' Education for the A.B. degree, the essence of exactness and the soul of propriety; Sister Maria Walburg (1924–1971), devoted to the classics, the first woman and the first sister to be elected an officer in the American Classical Society; Miss Gow (1927–1969), whose plays and verse choir were famed on and off campus, and whose speech students can still recite "Blow, bugle, blow. . ."; Sister Loyola Maria (1934–1971), academic dean and professor of Liturgy and Romance Languages, often striking terror in her students who nevertheless had fond memories of her; Sister Anne Xavier (1931–1971), devoted librarian;

Reverend August P. Vollmer, OSA, (1937–1971), chaplain and professor of German and Philosophy, whose very exact liturgies belied a gentle and understanding man; Sister Regina Dolores (1928–1972), opera and Glee Club director; Sister Marie de Sales (1925–1969), of Practice House fame; Sister Agnes Carmel Noel (1931–1969), who because of her work in the Cafeteria was hailed for "thirty-eight years of service to thousands of hungry college girls" ; Sister Anne Stanislaus (1936–1971), quiet and reflective professor of Latin and assistant registrar; Sister Francis Leo (1941–1971), artist and art critic; Sister Georgina (1927–1968), devoted to Fashion Design along with Sister Stella Bernard (1936–1972); Sister Eleanor Marie (1935–1972), who held the Chemistry Department to high standards; Sister Rose Martina (1933–1972), who brought laughter to the German Club and classes; and Dr. James Rowland (1929–1972), professor of History and Political Science. Father Thomas Lynch, a member of the faculty since 1933, died in 1963. His Irish wit, his knowledge of almost every literary work ever written, and his familiar greeting, "Hello girl [gurrl]," remain legendary.

Although some remained on campus in other posts, several sisters went to St. Joseph's Villa. Lay people returned to their homes, Boston for Miss Gow, who made an annual visit to the College almost until her death in 1985 at the age of ninety-five. Younger people replaced these long-term teachers. Students adjusted, but for alumnae it was difficult. Sister Mary Xavier remarked at the 1969 reunion, "We are living in an era of turbulence, and the winds of change are blowing to the college too. We all realize the suffering involved in change because it affects human lives. An old order does not fold its tent and quietly steal away. Sorrow and regret are but natural in a close-knit college community such as ours when the administration changes, beloved faculty members retire, and new appointments, new faces in old places, make old-time associations a little less familiar."

Sister Mary Xavier promised to keep faith with the past while pursuing every means of strengthening academics. In 1969 she announced a major in elementary education, opposed by some faculty members, who saw it as a weakening of the liberal arts curriculum. Yet it proved an asset when enrollment began to drop: this was imminent. A program of Continuing Education, at first just for women, began in September of 1969. They were a mature influence on traditional students and a great asset to the College. Men were admitted after January 1972, when an Evening Division was instituted under Dr. William Costello. Saturday and summer classes, reserved for only sisters since 1924, were now open to lay people, since the number of sisters attending these classes was falling dramatically. A cooperative program with Chestnut Hill Hospital School of Nursing was approved in September 1970. An exchange program with LaSalle College (now University), was very attractive to the young people at both schools, since neither was co-ed.

Meanwhile the entire curriculum was under study. The first major change came in 1970. A unit system replaced credits until 1974. The Language requirement was lessened by two semesters. Distributionals fell into the categories of Humanities, Social Sciences, and Natural Sciences; students could choose any course from within the group. Most controversial were the Religion and Philosophy requirements. Many felt that only two Theology courses, and Philosophy now buried in the Humanities, weakened the Catholic nature of the institution. Yet the change was made and the College remained Catholic.

These controversies were small in comparison to others that developed. In 1968 two young and attractive priests came on campus, Thomas Duggan, SJ, and John Sproule. They were filled with the spirit of Vatican II, held very popular, sometimes experimental liturgies. Crowds flocked to them. The two made friends and enemies very quickly. As student disturbances grew, they often found themselves at odds with the administration and some faculty, and on the side of the students. Many encounters centered around hiring and nonrenewal of contracts. Louise Bolger, Alumnae secretary since 1936, was urged to take a sabbatical. A controversial part-time Theology teacher's contract was not renewed. Father Duggan was not assigned a Religion course that students wanted; Father Shimkus was hired instead. Father Duggan left campus voluntarily; Father Sproule stayed on to fight these and similar battles, still popular with many students and some faculty until he returned to his native Canada in 1971.

Dr. and Mrs. Zenner, Father Vollmer, Father Lynch, Eleanor Burke Rowland, and Dr. James Rowland attend a dinner at the College.

An article in *The Inquirer* states, "About 200 students at Chestnut Hill College left their classes Wednesday afternoon [March 1, 1971] to demonstrate against the suspension of two freshmen for their "religious attitudes."[45] The two students had stolen into the Convent Chapel the previous evening, lit candles, and performed a mock religious ceremony, for which they were suspended. Others held a peaceful protest, encouraged by Father Sproule. The students were reinstated, after negotiations between the College administration and the Student Council. The administration "recognized the concern of the student body and the need for improved communication in the future."

Student Council minutes of 1970 reveal a lively interest in the theology controversy, reporting, "The statement *We feel the need for and are interested in a* Meaning of God *course to be taught by Father Duggan next semester* was

signed by 80% of [the group polled]." Students and administration conferred. Students responded that they "are not satisfied with this advisory and consultative role . . . [they] want a share in the decision-making and therefore request a radical change in policy and structure. . . . Chestnut Hill Students are assuming a new character which demands a new role. Chestnut Hill College Student Organization can only justify its existence in the implementation of its program."

They indeed had a new character. They were inquisitive; they discussed readily in and out of class; they challenged their professors to greater academic performance. They had initiative. They invited controversial speakers like Daniel Berrigan. They had film festivals with experimental art cinema: *Wild Strawberries, Eight and a Half.* For two years they held remarkable Arts Festivals, running everything from finances to clean-up. Directed by Alice McEnerney Cook, '70, Arts Festival '70 ran from March 4 to March 15, and included twenty-seven different events. Among them were folk singers and the Jean Williams dancers, a lecture by John Scali, ABC Washington news correspondent, and an indoor-outdoor

Father John Sproule interests his students in post–Vatican II theology.

sculpture exhibition from Washington, New York, and Philadelphia. Representatives from the mayor's and governor's office greeted the capacity crowds. The festival was a success from all angles, including financial.

Fournier News, the students said, is dead. As with May Day, this was no surprise. It had begun to deteriorate in the fifties, had a slight resurgence in the early sixties, but never reached its former stature. Students decided that the old method of objective journalism was passé; after two weeks, news is history. In January 1967, they began an experimental *Comment* mimeographed sheet, supplemented by a list of campus events. It survived until January 11, 1968, and voiced sometimes insightful, sometimes bitter, opinions. From November 6, 1970, to January 31, 1973, *One Small Voice* carried the news and views of the day. Also mimeographed, it evolved into a good vehicle of communication. It urged greater student involvement, condemned apathy, and agitated for the abolition of curfews and the legalization of smoking in the dormitories. Articles became progressively more positive.

Student-run, short-lived newspapers appeared. *Phoenix,* with three issues in 1974, contained mostly announcements, while *(parentheses)* in the spring of 1973, was an attempt at a literary magazine. Not as neat and organized as traditional publications,

115

Sister Maria Walburg Fanning was a revered professor of classics from 1924 to 1971.

Thomas Duggan, SJ, leads a popular liturgy in St. Joseph's Chapel.

they addressed issues rather than events. What was a loss to history was a gain for originality. The same fate befell the noble bird, *The Grackle*, reviving for only a brief time.

The young are impatient with lack of change; they expect it tomorrow. Many changes did come almost over night. In 1968, students served on the curriculum, rank and tenure, library, film, and lecture committees. Dormitory councils began in 1969. The dress code was lifted in 1970. Formal meals ended in 1971 when ARA took over the food service so loyally managed by Sister Francis Xavier with the help of the aging Nellie Scanlon and Margaret Houlihan, and Sisters St. Benedict, Mary Edgar McDermott, Agnes Carmel

Noel, St. Emily James. Sister Francis Xavier maintained her work with the Motherhouse until her sudden death in 1976; the others retired to new jobs. Holy water, curfew, and the sign-out book passed out of existence, and parental permissions for weekends were no longer required. Married students were allowed. All of these events made news in the local papers.

During the academic year 1970–1971 the administration, faculty, and student representatives met and met and met. They reflected and discussed students' demands. In May the Administrative Board concluded: "In order to establish confidence and trust among faculty, students, and administration, we have decided to establish a

Provisional College Council. . . . [It will include] two student representatives elected by the students. . . . By sharing in decision-making, students at Chestnut Hill will develop a sense of responsibility and maturity of judgment which will enable them to take their places as leaders in today's troubled world." In a bit more humorous vein, the Class of 1973 commented in their yearbook: "We lost a Jesuit and gained a College Council."

Students seemed satisfied. More tranquil days gradually appeared. After two very critical yearbooks, 1969 and especially 1970, emphasizing a College that was behind the times and unaware of social issues, that seemed to be rooted in a "clean fill" sign and preferred the Villa Fair to student needs, 1971 was positive and very much like the ones before 1968.

These students were alert and inquisitive, original and imaginative. But they were too few. Many factors contributed to a dramatic drop in enrollment. The disturbances on campus, the incertitude of direction, the apparent slowness of change, played a role. Another factor was the effect of Vatican II. Previously, Catholic students were required to attend a Catholic college. This policy remained alive throughout the fifties and early sixties, but Vatican II saw its demise. Chestnut Hill and its Catholic neighbors no longer had a captive audience. Active recruitment became necessary; Sister Editha became the first admissions director in 1970. Finally, the local men's colleges, LaSalle, Villanova, and St. Joseph's, decided to admit women. At first Chestnut Hill perceived this as no threat and was even consulted before the change. The College was confident of its population. In 1970, the incoming class numbered 123 residents and 89 day students. But the impact occurred almost immediately. If students came, many left after their first year. The exchange with LaSalle suffered because of coeducation. Community colleges became more prevalent, and were less expensive than Chestnut Hill, still a bargain at $2,600 for room, board, and tuition.

For the first time in its history, Chestnut Hill faced a declining enrollment. The Depression, the war, the postwar years all brought an increase. What these world shattering events failed to do, coeducation and the atmosphere of the sixties wrought. The Class of 1973 in their yearbook lament their diminishing numbers; by 1972 they were too few to fill Fournier.

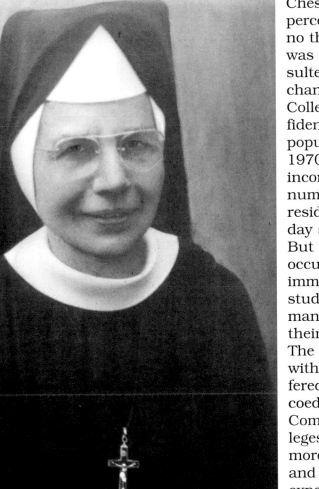

Sister Francis Xavier McPeak was everywhere on campus and seemed able to manage anything.

The Arts Festival of 1970 was a remarkable program, totally student-directed.

The College however found ingenious ways to increase enrollment: new programs already in place, as well as Early Childhood Education and Music Education approved in 1975; Montessori Education begun in 1972 with approval in 1978, and majors in American Studies and Classical Civilization. The revised calendar allowed for a month at Christmas time, permitting intersessions in France, England, and Marine Biology in Florida. The Interdisciplinary Honors Program, begun in 1968, was intensified to attract better students. High school seniors could take a course at the College, and Mount St. Joseph Academy instituted a program whereby honors seniors might have a full year of college courses while still sharing in their high school life.

Sister Mary Xavier describes the situation in her report to the congregational chapter of 1974: "Declining enrollment, escalating costs of instructional and maintenance services, faculty compensation, and inflation brought private colleges to what the Carnegie Commission described as the *peril*

point financially. Hovering on the marginal line between the black and the red each year, the college has operated on an austerity budget. All possible measures have been taken to shore up dwindling resources and increase our revenues." She also noted that faculty salaries rose 37 percent from 1968 to 1974. About fifty sisters resided at the College, but the numbers of lay faculty were growing rapidly. They were naturally very concerned about their salaries, which were then at the average norm. A 10 percent increase across the board was given for the 1971–1972 academic year. Tuition was increased from $1,400 in 1969 to $1,600 in 1972, to $1,800 in 1974. Room and board remained unchanged. However, the projected full-time enrollment for 1972–1973 was 475, down from 629. The result was a loss of $137,000, since 67 percent of the College revenue came from tuition.

Enrollment grew through a summer program, Action for Advancement, part of the Pennsylvania Act 101 Program. It began in 1972 for Hispanics who were financially and educationally disadvantaged and thus needed pre-college instruction. Ten young women were accepted, most from local schools. With tutoring and counseling it was hoped that they would reach the level required for acceptance. Two summer college courses permitted a lighter roster during their first year and thus insured a greater chance of success. All ten graduated from Chestnut Hill College. Thomas Kearns directed the program, assisted by Reverend John Donohie. The following year twenty students were accepted. The program was advertised as the only one of its kind for Hispanic women.

In December of 1974 the College received a letter from Harrisburg stating: "While I laud your effort to accommodate these students in terms of curriculum change and counseling attention, if your program is exclusively Spanish speaking and/or has a reputation of giving preferential acceptance to Spanish Surnamed individuals, you are in clear violation of Act 101 legislation and guidelines which direct services to be offered to economically and educationally disadvantaged students, without any ethnic preference."[46] This was a blow to the directors of the program, who had organized it exclusively for Hispanic students. All was not lost. The College immediately began to recruit other minorities. This ultimately helped to diversify the population, although there was a Hispanic majority for some time.

On the twentieth anniversary of Action for Advancement, Sister Mary Xavier returned and told the students, "Its success is your success story: approximately 400 educated, professional women have graduated through this program, making a difference in your own life, your families, and the human community as doctors, teachers, translators, researchers, social workers, dentists, podiatrists, church

workers, therapists, police women, lawyers, counselors, accountants, hotel managers and nutritionists. You are all out there, each and everyone, creating a better world. . . . You achieved your goals, and Chestnut Hill College's program has been formally recognized by Harrisburg as the best in the State."

Times such as these precluded any major building, but improvements and repairs continued, including a new generator and water tanks for St. Joseph's Hall. Students appreciated the redecoration of the cafeteria, and the relocation of the bookstore to the ground floor of St. Joseph's Hall. The new Coffee House next to the Cafeteria served as a gathering place and study room. It was popular for many years.

The West Parlor in St. Joseph's Hall, renamed the Redmond Room, honored Sister Catharine Frances Redmond. The furniture was seven-

The new "uniform" for students replaces skirts and dresses.

teenth-century French provincial style, with fleur-de-lis patterns in the rug, chosen for the congregational coat of arms. The paintings by Sister St. Luke Kelly were hung there to emphasize the heritage of the Sisters of St. Joseph. The Redmond Room was opened in 1971 for board meetings and formal occasions, and has seen many celebrities such as Beverly Sills, Mother Teresa, and Sioban McKenna.

Meanwhile Sister Catharine Frances herself was ill at nearby St. Joseph's Villa. On June 28, 1973, she died peacefully. Fifty graduates in cap and gown formed a guard of honor at her funeral, held on July 4 at Chestnut Hill. They stood in the Chapel, and along the path leading to the cemetery. It was a touching tribute to her, since many of them had interrupted their holiday week-end to be there. The fifty alumnae represented the fifty years of Chestnut Hill College, soon to be celebrated.

Sister Catharine Frances was born Elizabeth G. Redmond on December 18, 1898, the daughter of Edward and Frances McDevitt Redmond, a well-known family along the Main Line of suburban Philadelphia. Her parents died when she was very young, and a cousin took the three Redmond children into the Doyle family of successful landscapers. Sister attended Our Mother of Good Counsel School in Bryn Mawr, graduated from Catholic High School for Girls in 1915, and from normal school in 1917. She entered the Sisters of Saint Joseph on September 7, 1919. She taught at St. Bridget's and Mount Saint Joseph Academy before coming to the College in 1930. She received her B.A. from Villanova College in 1925, her M.A. in 1930 and her Ph.D. in 1936 from the University of Pennsylvania. Her dissertation was entitled *The Convent School of French Origin in the United States: 1727–1843.* During her years at Chestnut Hill, she was active in outside professional activities.

Looks might be deceiving in one's effort to evaluate her as a person. Sister Patrick Marie observed, "A very slow-moving person, she gave the impression of not knowing what was going on, yet never, never try to fool her!" She seemed to know when or when not to intervene. She was a firm believer in freedom both for students and faculty. Sister Harriet Corrigan observes that she allowed students to work through to a decision themselves. If she disapproved, she would say why, then let the students continue, but they must accept the responsibility.

Dr. Lukacs praises her as a woman with common sense and earthly wisdom. He especially approved of her moderate expansion in the sixties, noting that the College could have been saddled with an enormous debt if she had built more than absolutely needed. Her devoted assistant, Miss Alice Corcoran was deeply loyal to her and noted "the open door" in the president's office; anyone was welcome at any time.

Sister Catharine Frances was a generous person. She would give no-interest loans to needy faculty members. When times were good, she gave a Christmas bonus to the lay faculty. She helped needy students, especially those in Third World countries, such as Nigeria and Biafra, and supported the missions. She was also a shrewd negotiator. Lay faculty met with her on a one-to-one basis to discuss salaries. She was as generous as possible.

Sister Catharine Frances is remembered less as a teacher than as an administrator. Her voice was soft and somnolent, putting students to sleep in class but at ease in a tense situation. The same might be said for faculty at meetings. Yet she was an educator in the strict sense of the word. The *Alumnae Bulletin* of 1969 pays tribute to her on her retirement, "In all her work, Sister exemplified for her students the ideals with which she sought to inspire them. Particularly did she instill in them the philosophy that dominated her whole life: that woman's life is one of loving service, to her God, to herself, to her family and to all whom her life touches."

It was her warmth and friendliness

The Act 101 Board along with Sister Mary Xavier Kirby (standing, second from right) begin the program in 1972.

that students and alumnae appreciated the most. These words appear most frequently in the tributes sent to her at the time of her resignation in 1968. Her letter of October 4, 1958, celebrating the centenary of the Sisters of Saint Joseph at Chestnut Hill, and of Mount Saint Joseph Academy, expresses her philosophy for the students and the College: "You are carrying on the spirit and the tradition of the Sisters of Saint Joseph who for more than three centuries have devoted themselves to the education of women, following the axiom of our Congregation, *that on the education of women largely depends the future of society.*"

In her last presidential report, given at the fall alumnae reunion in 1968, she said, "These six years [1962–1968] cover a period of difficult but challenging times in the history of education. They were turbulent and often destructive years on many American campus-

es, years of unacademic attitudes. They will be remembered as a time of change and revolution in the history of American higher education and of Chestnut Hill College." These prophetic words proved all too true, and would extend beyond 1968. By the time of her death, the flood waters were receding. At Christmastime, faculty and administration rose early to admire the elegant decorations. Camelot had come to Chestnut Hill College. But most surprising was the Bulletin Board. The seniors of the class of 1972 said that "In all the world there is not a more perfect spot than *here* at Camelot." Their four years at Chestnut Hill had been Camelot. It was like the dove emerging from Noah's ark—there was new life!

121

Betty Buckley, devoted physical education teacher, ready for
archery, tennis, basketball, or hockey!

CHAPTER TEN
NEW LIFE

New life there was, although it was only in retrospect that the College community recognized it. Chestnut Hill was approaching its jubilee: fifty years of service, survival, success. Jubilees are times of reflection, of re-evaluation, of rejoicing. As the College prepared a grandiose celebration, it found itself re-examining the past in the light of the future. For fifty years it proclaimed itself a small, Catholic, liberal arts college for women. Did this mean the same thing in 1974 as it meant in 1924?

In 1924 Mount Saint Joseph was a college for women by destiny. In 1974 it was a college for women by choice. Church-related colleges were exclusively male or female. Women's colleges arose because women were not welcomed in higher education. Even when they were, church authorities frowned on coeducation as a corruption of morals and a reversal of the traditional subservient role of women. Women emerged from the first all-female colleges as independent and assertive. Early women's colleges were champions of women's rights, feminists before the term was invented.[47] Mount Saint Joseph College, as heir to this tradition, found less need to proclaim its feminism than to live it.

By 1974, coeducation became the norm. Men's colleges began to accept women. Women's colleges like Chestnut Hill found themselves losing enrollment. They desperately fought for survival. Neighboring colleges, Holy Family, Our Lady of Angels (now Neumann), Cabrini, Gwynedd Mercy, chose the route of coeducation. Although Chestnut Hill accepted men through Continuing Education, it chose to remain a woman's college for its traditional age students, albeit facing some controversy among faculty and students. This was a deliberate choice, with obvious consequences. It needed to redefine its mission, prove the advantages of a woman's college, and enrich the curriculum through courses that emphasized women.

Students in the late seventies showed much greater interest in women's issues. Feminism was in the air since the mid-sixties. Women speakers emphasized women and careers. In contrast to the attitude of the fifties that highlighted women in their family role, articles in *Kaleidoscope* in the late seventies studied the Equal Rights Amendments and its positive implications for women, and spoke against sex discrimination.

Chestnut Hill was also a Catholic college, which welcomed all religions. The first lay faculty members were all practicing Catholics; Sister Maria Kostka had insisted on this. As time went on, qualified non-Catholic lay people applied to Chestnut Hill. They found their beliefs in harmony with the mission of the College, and contributed greatly to the academic life. As the enrollment crisis necessitated a broader market, student applications of other faiths and of no particular faith came to Chestnut Hill. What did it mean to be a Catholic college? In 1973–1974, the Catalogue reads: "As a

JUBILEE LOGO

1924-1974

DESIGNED BY
CONSTANCE McCARTHY BOYLAN

The Jubilee Logo, designed by Constance McCarthy Boylan, emphasizes tradition and the future.

Catholic institution, Chestnut Hill College promotes the growth of the whole person, for from a Christian perspective, the student is encouraged not only in scholarship, but also in social services to [others]."

Finally, the liberal arts tradition needed re-examination. In 1928, there were many opportunities open to Liberal Arts graduates, especially teaching. During the Depression years, women found work where and if they could, their college diploma sometimes an asset. The war brought science into the fore, and postwar years emphasized marriage rather than career. The Liberal Arts taught women how to live rather than to earn a living. Yet many of these women found themselves back in college classes in the 1970s. They too needed a job for income and for fulfillment. Chestnut Hill responded with new majors, Business Education in 1977 and Business Administration in 1980. Several CED classes emphasized the practical: Thacher Longstreth, president of the Greater Philadelphia Chamber of Commerce, taught a course on planned renewal of city areas. A. Charles Peruto taught Principles of Law; Milton Goldberg, Current Trends in Early Childhood Education. Not only did they bring a practical dimension to the curriculum; they also added prestige.

In 1977, under the direction of Sister Mary Kieran, the College held a science update for thirty women scientists, among them nineteen alumnae, to prepare them for re-entry into the job market. The same year, Women in Management began to equip students for the business world. In 1976 the College received a $26,000 federal grant from the Department of Health, Education, and Welfare for cooperative education under Career Services Director Carmela Palermo. A student could spend a semester full-time out in the real market place while earning college credits. Still the liberal arts remained at the core of the curriculum, so that students could practice what Sister Maria Kostka had told the Depression classes: "You will earn a living, because you must. But you are here to learn how to live."

Sister Maria Kostka's memory remained alive. In 1971, during Alumnae Weekend, transferred to May because of the revised academic calendar, the Library was dedicated in her honor, now called *Logue Library*. The celebration on May 22 consisted of welcome speeches by Sister Mary Xavier and Mother Alice Anita Murphy, chair of the Board of Directors,[48] and an address by Edward Logue. A Eucharistic Liturgy closed the day. Gruber Theater was named for the family of Sister Rita Madeleine (Anne Gruber, '30), and the Reference Room for the Alumnae, in recognition of their generous contributions. In her address, Sister Mary Xavier said,"It is indeed fitting that this library be named for [Sister Maria Kostka], for, as a great educator she fully realized that the library is the heart of the college. Its development

David Contosta enriches the College through his teaching and scholarship.

and expansion were her constant concern. And because you members of the alumnae, her former students, caught the enthusiasm of her desire to acquire the finest collection of books and to provide adequate facilities for research, through your fund-raising efforts, you have contributed in great measure to the fulfillment of her dream."

Sister Maria Kostka loved books, and the Library that housed them. She combated provincialism and expected students to move beyond the campus. When she requested that Mount St. Joseph be renamed Chestnut Hill College in 1938, she did so because of her sense of place; a college should be part of the community where it was located. A real integration, however, was only to begin in the 1970s.

Chestnut Hill was an exclusive section of Philadelphia, dominated by white, Anglo-Saxon Episcopalians. The idea of associating with a college considered a training school for nuns was unthinkable in pre-Vatican II days. Dr. Lukacs recalls introducing himself to a friend of his future wife, and saying that he taught at Chestnut Hill. The person thought he meant Chestnut Hill Academy; he had never heard of the College.[49] The Augustinians from Our Mother of Consolation served at the College and the Motherhouse, and Marie Reinhart Jones, '47, edited the *Chestnut Hill Local*, but there were few other connections.

In 1967, the Villa Fair, so much criticized by students in 1969, was held on the College grounds. The *Chestnut Hill Local*[50] reports that over 135,000 visited the Fair from September 20 to 23 and caused massive traffic jams. "The brain trust of the order, the nuns who hold doctorates and teach at Chestnut Hill College, were in charge of balloons," the article continued. Sister Mary Xavier, to be named president within the year, had her picture in the *Evening Bulletin* selling balloons. Among the visitors were members of the Chestnut Hill Community, many of whom came to the campus for the first time.

Sister Mary Xavier's balloon venture took flight in an enduring association between the Chestnut Hill Community Association and the College. In 1970, she began discussions with Alfred Steele, president of the Chestnut Hill Hospital Board of Trustees, and J. Dan Miller, hospital administrator, to discuss affiliation of the hospital with the College. Alfred Steele became a member of the Chestnut Hill Board of Directors when the College changed the name and the composition of the Board. In 1975, Chestnut Hill College students had a booth at the Main Street Fair, held annually for the benefit of the Hospital. They sold articles made of recycled materials, and called their booth E-COLLEGE-E. In 1977 the Fair was held on the College campus, and the annual Friends of the Wissahickon horses and carriages paraded through the campus for many years. As a culmination to her efforts, in 1976 Sister Mary Xavier received the Woman of the Year Award from the Chestnut Hill Business and Professional Women's Club in 1976.

Other faculty helped further this association. Sister Grace Miriam became a member of the Chestnut Hill Community Association Board in 1972 as principal of Our Mother of Consolation School. Sisters Mary Xavier and future presidents were also members. Sister Harriet P. Corrigan, '54, served as Democratic Committee woman, and member of the Board of the Chestnut Hill Historical Society, where she was also influential in placing college students as interns. Sister Consuelo Maria was the first president of the Cascade Aphasia Center, located in Chestnut Hill. Sister Ann Edward gave countless lectures to groups in the area. David Contosta, professor of History, was to contribute through his book, *Suburb in the City*. And of course there was Father Casey, who with his dog and his own personality, brought enormous growth to ecumenical and friendly relations between the College, the Catholic Church, and the Chestnut Hill Community.

The Chestnut Hill Community was a significant part of the Golden Jubilee

Celebration. On December 17, 1974, eight outstanding citizens were honored, and received special medals. They were John W. Bodine, former president of the Academy of Natural Sciences of Philadelphia; Madeleine K. Butcher, president of the Chestnut Hill Community Association; Reverend John F. Casey, OSA, pastor of Our Mother of Consolation parish; Edith Emerson, curator of Woodmere Art Gallery; Thacher Longstreth, president of the Greater Philadelphia Chamber of Commerce and PENJERDEL; Eleanor Potter, former headmistress of Springside School; George L. Spaeth, eye surgeon; and Lloyd P. Wells, founder and developer of the Chestnut Hill Realty Trust and Chestnut Hill Community Association, who gave the address at the event.

In her remarks to the honorees, Sister Mary Xavier stated, "No other college in the City of Philadelphia, in the State, or even in the Nation, can boast of so felicitous a setting. No other community, I'm sure, can offer its college the rich resources of One Marvelous Mile, extending from Northwestern Avenue to Chestnut Hill Avenue, which contains within it a liberal arts college, an arboretum, an art gallery, a private academy, a conference center, a hospital, a library and four churches. Indeed this *is* a community vitally concerned with things of the mind and spirit."

A year of Jubilee was the time to boast of the "one Marvelous Mile." The Jubilee was a year in the making (1973–1974) and a year in the celebrat-

Alumnae and faculty experience Latin hospitality in a pre-Jubilee Puerto Rican trip.

ing (1974–1975). At commencement exercises on May 12, Chestnut Hill College awarded its first honorary degrees to Dr. Alma Dea Morani, plastic surgeon, and John Gurash, chair of the Board of INA Corporations, who boasted that he was the first CHC alumnus. Special scholarships were awarded to applicants during the Jubilee year, funded by generous gifts from alumnae.

Meanwhile, committee chairs planned a year to remember. Sister Ann Edward was general chair. Charles G. Simpson was chair of the Board of Directors; John T. Lyons, publicity; Mary Kay Schubert Denny, '40, publications; Constance McCarthy Boylan, '40, art; Roseanita Schubert Coffey, '49, dance; Blanche Haviland Moore, '50, alumnae participation with Mary Nagle Bell, '54, co-chair. The events involved everyone: city and church officials, alumnae, students, administration, faculty, and friends.

The celebration began on September 22, 1974, fifty years to the day when the first fifteen students entered Mount Saint Joseph College. John Cardinal Krol celebrated a solemn Mass at 3:00 p.m. at the Cathedral of Sts. Peter and Paul, filled with dignitaries, alumnae, faculty, students, and friends. Dr. Peter and Mrs. (Ida Rosa, '36) Pugliese planned this event. Over twelve hundred people attended the open-air reception in front

Sister Ann Edward Bennis (left), chair of the Jubilee Celebration, joins Sister Mary Xavier Kirby to receive Mayor Frank Rizzo's welcome.

of the Philadelphia Museum of Art, under a cloudless September sky. Similar celebrations took place at Boston College, Massachusetts, at Georgetown University, and San Gabriel Mission in California. At the Cathedral in Philadelphia, Alumnae President Ellen Whiteside Byrne, '56, presented a box at the Offertory, containing the names of every student who had ever attended the College.

The year was filled with great events. The Art Buchwald lecture on November 12, 1974, and the Beverly Sills concert on January 17, 1975, still stand out as most memorable. Five members of the first graduating class, Marie Keffer Avil, Helen Greeve Davaney, Eleanor Dolan Egan, Sisters Irene Marie O'Connor and Katherine Aurelia Maginn received medals from Sister Alice Anita, chair of the Board of Directors. On March 15, 1975, eleven Sisters of St. Joseph were honored. They had taught in the College on Saturdays and in the summer, but were never full-time faculty. Recipients were Sisters Anna Josephine, Claire Helene, Felicitas, Martin Anthony, Mary Dennis, Miriam de Sales, Pauline, Rita Francis, San José, St. Ignatius, and St. Alice. Reverend Raymond Brown was the speaker. Both he and the honorees were extremely popular, and guests filled the Auditorium to overflowing.

Under leaders Marilyn Sweeney, Mellie O'Donnell, Pat O'Donnell, and

Sisters John Gertrude Steckbeck, Patricia O'Donnell, Ann Michael Joyce, Catherine Knobbs, Dolores Malecka, and Rosemary Scheirer mount the Art Museum steps for the outdoor celebration on September 22, 1974.

Karen Anderson, students raised $3,000 by raffling off a car, won by football star Randy Logan. On December 7, they presented a sparkling Christmas concert, which began in the Auditorium and, reminiscent of early days, moved across campus where it continued in the Rotunda with Benjamin Britten's "Ceremony of the Carols," and ended in Fournier with a viewing of the decorations. On February 19, they organized a student-alumnae day, and hosted over one hundred alumnae. The day included a session with students leaders on "CHC Today." It ended with a talk by John Lukacs on the history of the College.

The year ended with The Golden Gala, Saturday, May 17, 1975, at the Bellevue Stratford Hotel, with music by Peter Duchin and his Orchestra. Over six hundred attended, and enjoyed the pre-dinner reception and a surprise appearance of the Philadelphia Mummers. The grand finale was the descending chandelier in the Grand Ballroom, miraculously transformed into a Maypole! Eight former May Queens were present, and proved that they could still twine those streamers. On a more solemn note, the week-end and the festivities came to a close with a liturgy celebrated by Bishop Fulton J. Sheen, followed by a witty and inspiring talk at the brunch. And on a financially happy note, the Alumnae presented the College with $130,000,

Doris Kelly, Constance McCarthy Boylan, Sister Mary Xavier Kirby, and Dr. Pugliese admire the Jubilee commemorative plate outside the Art Museum.

Sister Mary Xavier Kirby, far left, welcomes Beverly Sills (second from left) and other guests to the Jubilee Concert.

almost half of their goal of $300,000 by 1976. Jubilee contributions added over $12,000 to the Endowment Fund.

The *Alumnae Bulletin* of 1975, from which much of this material was gleaned, contains excerpts from letters solicited by the editors. They note: "There proved to be a striking continuity of attitude in the Chestnut Hill College woman. Reasons for choosing the College remained unchanged throughout the years, predominantly because it is small, because it is Catholic, because it is administered by the Sisters of St. Joseph whose teaching had been found excellent in high school, whether in the 1920s or the 1970s. . . . The desire for learning was more often stressed with the older graduates. A specific career figures in the objectives of more recent graduates, but it is a matter of emphasis only. . . . The one theme that stood out above all the others was that education at Chestnut Hill had enriched their lives. The caring of the faculty for them as individuals had developed their abilities and their confidence in themselves, and taught them to strive for excellence in all things. They had learned sound fundamental values that could be applied to living any life."

As the seventies were soon to give way to the eighties and nineties, there was optimism in the air at the College. The enrollment was rising; the deficit was dropping. After two anxious years in the red, the budget was, as Sister Mary Xavier said, comparing it to the shade of her stockings, "barely black."

The increased number of students brought a new problem—they all wanted to be residents! In 1972, there were 233 residents; in 1979, 368. Room space grew by using the Senior Lounge in Fournier and the former student organization offices on the ground floor of Fontbonne as bedrooms. Finally in 1979, classrooms on the second floor of Clement Hall were sacrificed to rooms for residents. In one of the rare moves back to the future, they returned to classrooms in 1985 when the resident population decreased, and thus they remain—for the moment.

Enrollment was also growing, but not fast enough. The sister student population dropped from 643 in 1969 to 113 in 1979. Sisters had kept summer and Saturday classes alive since 1924. Although their happy chatter on Saturday mornings awakened many a resident, they integrated well with students and formed many enduring friendships when some came as full-time students in the early seventies. One of the goals in the foundation of the College was the education of the sisters, often a long process since all were part-time students and full-time teachers. The goal was now attained sooner and better, and newer programs filled the void.

Meanwhile the traditional students were changing. Sister Mary Xavier described them as "the now generation giving way to the tomorrow people" when she addressed the alumnae in 1974. They returned to some of the

Sister Katherine Aurelia Maginn, '28, receives her Jubilee medal as Sisters Clare Joseph, Helen Veronica, Paul Daniel, Alice Anita, Georgina, Mary Xavier, and Loyola Maria look on.

traditions of the past: kept Christmas, gradually resurrected clubs as "interest groups," formed a singing group known as "Looking Glass," and following the movements of the late sixties, put great emphasis on involvement. Bread for the World, Walk for Guatemala, Rice Bowl, Thanksgiving and Christmas collections for the poor were among their commitments. In 1976 the Biology Department and the American Chemical Society sponsored a Women and Cancer Forum. Volunteers helped at St. John's Hospice for homeless and hungry men. They participated in the Cardinal's Commission for Human Relations, Toys for Tots, and Catholic Relief Services. They became more aware of world hunger. A seminar "Focus on Hunger," in April of 1979, included a fast for the benefit of the starving poor.

Although the resident population increased greatly, the campus as the center of student life faded. The seventies and eighties brought more mobility. Cars crowded the campus; parking became a problem. The campus became a deserted village on weekends. Not all departures from campus were for entertainment, however. Inflation gripped the country, tuition costs were rising, and students had to work. Many held part-time jobs in the evenings and on week-ends. Others worked on campus to help defray expenses.

Changing schedules and off-campus departures had an impact on sports. Miss Buckley reports, "In 1977–1978 more games were added to the limited number. While this increased the interest of the participants and produced more varied competition, it made undefeated seasons hard to come by. Tournament and Conference championships thus supplanted the undefeated season as a measure of a team's superiority. In 1978 Chestnut Hill won the title in volleyball and, in 1981, the ANC tournament. The softball team won the Conference championship three years in a row (1979–1981)."[51]

Naturally, students were interested

in their future. College had to prepare them both to earn a living and to learn how to live. Thus many seminars and lectures addressed this issue. In November of 1976, students participated in an all-day seminar for Female Heads of Household, with Northwest Center and the Medical College of Pennsylvania. Mary Alice Duffy,'50, spoke. Students held a Social Work Day in October of 1978 and a Career Conference on November 18, 1978. Among the speakers was Marjorie Rendell, whose husband was to become mayor of Philadelphia in the nineties.[52] She returned as commencement speaker in 1999. In 1979 a Career Conference for Science took place, and other departments held similar events.

To help prepare students for the real world, a dual degree program with the College of Allied Health Sciences of Thomas Jefferson Hospital began in 1978. At the same time, a cooperative program with Villanova University for Catholic Elementary School Principals attracted both religious and lay principals. Chief Operating Officer of ITT, Francis J. Donleavy organized a unique course called Corporate Decision Making in 1979. It was team-taught by a group of business executives, focusing on the long-range goals of a fictional company. Many important business people of the area participated, and later provided useful contacts for future graduates. Internships began, and gave students an opportunity to experience the world of work before full-time employment, and often provided a point of entry into a company.

Yet the mission of learning how to live and how to think continued. John Lukacs founded the History School, unique at Chestnut Hill, through a $48,000 grant from the National Endowment for the Humanities and received high praise for his unusual idea. Students took a minimum of six historically oriented courses within their major field. At the conclusion of the program, they took a special seminar and received a certificate. In the tradition of the liberal arts, students

129

Bishop Sheen is welcomed to the College by Sister Mary Xavier Kirby for the liturgical closing of the Jubilee Year.

trained in cause and effect, in chronological detail, and in probing reasons for actions, proved a real asset to any business or profession.

In 1975, the College could boast of fifty alumnae physicians, six lawyers, 565 Master's Degrees and thirty-one doctorates. One Chestnut Hill graduate was a professor at Harvard, and many others were teaching and conducting research at the college level. Among the most highly publicized alumnae was Kathleen M. Donohue Byerly, '66, who made the cover of *Time* magazine on January 5, 1976, as one of twelve Women of the Year. In 1976 she was a lieutenant commander, USN, a management specialist, and the first woman to serve as an aide and flag secretary to an admiral. She oversaw a staff of fifty-five and three Navy commands: San Diego, Hawaii, Japan. She was commencement speaker at Chestnut Hill College in 1976.

Other Chestnut Hill students toured the world while still in college. The Intersession programs to England and France continued. In 1974, Sister Josephine Rucker, '36, inaugurated a Year Abroad Program in Salzburg, Austria, with the assistance of Dr. Liselotte Widmann, a professor at the University of Salzburg and a former Fulbright lecturer at the College. The first students profited intellectually and culturally. Unfortunately the program was abandoned in 1979 for insufficient registration. In 1977, a French Program was instituted in cooperation with the *Cours de civilisation française de la Sorbonne.* It has continued successfully, with students from other colleges often joining Chestnut Hill.

Faculty members also traveled abroad more frequently. Sister Irma Mercedes (Mary Helen Kashuba, '55) spent the summer of 1973 at Moscow State University on a grant for American professors of Russian. Dr. Lester Conner was appointed assistant director of the Yeats International Summer School in Sligo, Ireland, where he had taught since 1967. He had been visiting professor at Trinity College, Dublin, Ireland, in 1971–1972. Ireland became a special focus at Chestnut Hill, with the donation of an authentic replica of the ninth-century *Book of Kells* by the widow of Judge Clare Gerald Fenerty in 1970. Books given by Lester Conner and Father Thomas Lynch were added to form the Irish Collection, housed in the Irish Room in Logue Library, which continues to receive donations.

The broader world came to Chestnut Hill. Perhaps the most outstanding visit was in 1976, when Mother Teresa of Calcutta came to the College. Marie Jones in the *Chestnut Hill Local*, August 12, 1976, describes the visit: "At the college, Mother, who seems at ease with all people, no matter how high or low their station, was greeted by a delighted group of SSJ nuns. When she saw them waiting for her . . . she gave her familiar prayer sign, flashed her glowing smile, and then greeted each one individually, taking their hands in both of hers." Her state funeral in 1997 brought back memories of this highlighted event.

As new life came to the College, older members of the faculty continued to retire. Retirement was now compulsory at age sixty-seven for faculty and administration, although part-time was permitted until age seventy-two. Many sisters remained at the College in other capacities. Such was Sister Jane Frances Duffy, who had a kind word and a generous touch for everyone. She had come in 1939 "in delicate health, and therefore was given twelve hours of math, ten hours of religion, Saturday and summer school, and corridor duty."[53] In 1973 she became financial consultant, and only in 1992 really retired to St. Joseph's Villa, where she died in 1993. Sister Mary Julia Daly (1931–1977) remained as artist in residence until 1993 when she too left the College and continued her artistic work at St. Joseph's Villa until her death in 1999. Sister Patrick Marie Flood taught Chemistry from 1945 to 1975, when she became director of Development until 1983. Sister Miriam Elizabeth McCoy retired in 1974 after guiding the Biology Department to rival Chemistry. Sister Helen de Sales Forrest (1938–1975), died shortly after her retirement. In 1977 Dr. William Costello, professor and director of Continuing Education retired after twenty-eight years of service, as did Betty Buckley, Physical Education Department chair for thirty-five years. She returned frequently to the campus to prepare her *History of Physical Education at Chestnut Hill*. John B. Rey retired to his museum-like home in Philadelphia in 1979 after twenty-nine years. Miss Alice Corcoran went from

Students play field hockey on the new field in the 1970s.

years as social dean in 1941, to administrative assistant, to the French Department. In 1975 she retired to her comfortably renovated barn in Penn Yan, New York, to a quiet life punctuated by her traditional trips to France until her death in 1987.

Another retirement was noteworthy, although not after decades of service. Sister Margaret Fleming, '56, Student Council president, had the marks of future leadership as a college student, years, she says, that she thoroughly enjoyed. She became dean of students in 1968, just in time to handle the challenges of the late sixties and early seventies. This she did with great astuteness, always respecting the individual. Students likewise respected her. In 1979 the senior class chose her as graduation speaker. The student newspaper, *Kaleidoscope,* noted that this was rather unusual, but then, Sister Margaret Fleming was an unusual dean of students. She gave an inspiring address with rain pelting down on the roof of the outdoor tent. The following summer the congregational chapter

Sister Margaret Fleming, '56, was dean of students (1968–1979) and superior general of the Sisters of St. Joseph (1989–1999).

elected her to the administration of the congregation, and in 1989 she became superior general. A great honor to the College, and a tribute to those students who noted that she was indeed unusually expert. In her letter announcing Sister's election, Sister Mary Xavier noted, "The high morale of the students and their positive feelings for the College are attributable in large measure to her affection and concern for each one of them and to her very special charism for creating harmonious interpersonal relationships."

The academic year 1979–1980 began with a new dean of students, Sister Adele Solari, '55. It also began with campus improvements, such as the smokestack, renovation of the pantry, new food service equipment, renovation and addition of faculty offices, and lighting in the parking lot. Fournier was now fifty years old, and St. Joseph's Hall seventy-five. They began to need more and more attention; this has remained a pressing problem. Although the enrollment was

John Lukacs directs the History School through an NEH grant.

growing, so was the lay faculty and so was inflation.

Sister Mary Xavier realized the challenges of the eighties. The impending discontinuation of the Collaborative Nursing Program[54] required new ventures. Lowered enrollment, fewer sisters, a different student population, in short a different world was emerging. The stability of the past was rapidly giving way to the mobility of the future. The computer age had begun. Fundraising was a pressing need. Rising enrollment was only a temporary phenomenon. Yet basically, the picture was bright. Faculty and students were content. The College was debt free and in the black. As Sister Mary Xavier herself had stated in her report to the Chapter: "Academically, the last five years have been years of new direc-

tions and options, new or expanded programs, as well as additional affiliations with other institutions. . . . The College has achieved purposeful stability in the present."

In a move that took everyone by surprise, first of all the Board of Directors, Sister Mary Xavier wrote to the chair of the Board, Sister Dorothea Newell: "With this new decade, Chestnut Hill College enters upon an era of tremendous change and challenge, one that will demand a kind of leadership vastly different from that of the 70s. I am convinced, therefore, that this is the appropriate time for a change in the leadership of the College. Accordingly, I wish to submit my resignation as President and to request you to initiate the process necessary to choose my successor." Wisely, she realized that success is short-lived, and that it is better to leave willingly on the crest of the wave than to be swept out to sea.

In accepting Sister Mary Xavier's resignation, Sister Dorothea Newell noted, "It is better for all concerned that there be a change of Administration when the times are good for that institution, rather than when it is a time of crisis. These are good times for Chestnut Hill College. For us, it is not necessary, indeed, hardly possible to list Sister Mary Xavier's remarkable achievements." Her accomplishments were many. She received glowing tributes from far and wide. Perhaps the alumnae bulletin, *Update*, from spring 1980 sums it up best: "In her twelve years as president, the fourth in the College's fifty-six year history, Sister Mary Xavier more than fulfilled the Alumnae Association's greeting to her as she took office. 'CHC has always had a president exactly right for the times.' In a period marked by campus unrest nationally and grave financial problems for higher education, Sister guided CHC in an innovative, program-oriented administration, and leaves it financially in the black, academically in place for the 1980s, and clearly identifiable as a Catholic woman's college of high quality."

Sister Mary Xavier Kirby welcomes Mother Teresa of Calcutta (left) to the College in 1976.

Lorraine Busch gives the very young an experience of the water in the Summer Arts Camp.

Chapter Eleven
Mobility

Sister Mary Xavier Kirby had indicated the need for a new type of leadership in the eighties. This was the time of shared decision-making and consultation. In the past the Congregational Council, on the Board of Directors, chose the president. As Sisters of St. Joseph, they knew the potential candidate well. Like some arranged marriages, their choice miraculously succeeded. The Board was now composed both of sisters and lay people. They were to participate, along with everyone in the College community.

A Search Committee represented members of the Board. All eligible Sisters of St. Joseph could submit their candidacy. Eight applied: Sisters Harriet Corrigan, George Edward Conway, Catherine Knobbs, Irma Mercedes Kashuba, Kathryn Miller, Matthew Anita MacDonald, Patricia O'Donnell, and Sheila Marie Scheirer. Meetings of administration, faculty, staff, students, alumnae focused on the desired qualities in the candidate. All wanted a Sister of St. Joseph, a unifier and a communicator, the chief ceremonial officer of the College. She was to engage in long-range planning, work for the professional development of the faculty, and make contacts with the wider world. The Search Committee asked the candidates to assess the present state of the College, express their vision for the eighties, and define the mission of a Catholic college. Despite the difficulty of the task, they chose the right person for the right time: Sister Matthew Anita MacDonald. The entire College community immediately welcomed her.

Sister Matthew Anita (Joann MacDonald, '60) was the first alumna president. Like Sister Catharine Frances Redmond she held a doctorate in the history and philosophy of Education, also from the University of Pennsylvania. She taught English in the high schools of Philadelphia, and

Education at Chestnut Hill from 1969 to 1970. From 1970 to 1973 she served as assistant academic dean and from 1975 to 1980 directed the Continuing Education Division. In 1973 she obtained an American Council on Education Fellowship in Academic Administration. The following year she worked with Mary Patterson McPherson, then dean of the under-graduate division at Bryn Mawr College and later president. This year enriched her both professionally and personally, and Dr. McPherson remained her good friend and mentor.

Warmth and friendliness to students and alumnae were to characterize her administration. She would display many of the same qualities as Sister Catharine Frances, known for her one-to-one dealings with people. She had similar training, coming from an administrative background with English and Education. Both had a long association with the College, and came after challenging times.

Sister Matthew's was the first formal inauguration, held at 3:00 p.m. on Thursday, October 23, 1980. The academic procession included faculty, board members, students, alumnae, and representatives of other colleges. A member of each group spoke. Dr. McPherson gave the keynote address. In her inaugural address Sister Matthew accepted the challenges that awaited her. Then guests, faculty, and students celebrated. The day was even a holiday from classes.

The eighties were to remain challenging times. Some were obvious: enrollment was to drop, as predicted in the late seventies. With coeducation very desirable and the number of college-age students diminishing, recruitment was crucial. Inflation was raging everywhere, as a result of the Iranian oil crisis. Money was never plentiful at Chestnut Hill; what saved the day was the contributed services of the sisters. Though still numerous, their numbers were slowly eroding. More lay people joined the faculty, staff members increased, and with tuition still providing over 65 percent of income, fund-raising would be a priority. Fournier and St. Joseph's Hall were aging, and repairs were imperative and costly.

Previously faculty and administration were stable. The dean of students was Sister Catharine Frances throughout most of Sister Maria Kostka's thirty years, Sister Gertrude Leonore Lanman for Sister Catharine Frances' twelve, and Sister Margaret Fleming for eleven of Sister Mary Xavier Kirby's twelve years. Three deans in fifty-five years were followed by four deans in twelve years: Sisters Adele Solari from 1979 to 1981; Frances Hart from 1981 to 1987, Genevieve Prendergast from 1987 to 1991, and Mary Josephine Larkin until 1996, when she became dean of the Library and Information Resources.

Before 1980, all sisters lived on campus, although contrary to popular belief, did not all think alike. A number then moved to St. Michael's Hall, the former Residence Hall, to make room for resident students and to experience a more meaningful community life in the spirit of Vatican II. After the need for student housing waned, the sisters still chose smaller communities. Some elected a short stay at the College, contrary to their predecessors.

Sister Matthew Anita MacDonald, '60, became the fifth president of the College in 1980.

Sister Clare Joseph O'Halloran was registrar from 1926 until 1969. During Sister Matthew Anita's term, there were three registrars: Sisters Grace Margaret Rafferty until her 1983 retirement, Rose David Iseminger until her sudden death in 1988, and Catharine Fee until her appointment as associate dean in 1997. The registrar was a powerful force in Sister Clare Joseph's time, directing the sisters' studies for the A.B. Degree and graduate study. The academic dean assumed many of these duties. Sister Kathryn Miller was the only one for thirteen years. She maintained the integrity of the curriculum and introduced new and timely majors: Computer and Mathematical Sciences, Accounting, and Molecular Biology in 1985, and Fine Arts in 1990. Sister Elaine Cullen, a stable treasurer, kept finances afloat from 1981 to 1994.

Other people came and went. Sabbaticals became more frequent; Lester Conner went to Ireland in 1981. In 1986–1987, he changed places with John O'Dougherty, and taught in suburban Dublin. After the sisters received tenure in 1986, they too received sabbatical leaves and moved across the country and the world.

Maintenance and Housekeeping staff also saw changes; the familiar faces of John Brady, Cliff, Ed, Jim Brooks, Ellen and others gave way to professional service organizations, with quick turnover. One of the longest and most faithful was Leroy Steptoe, who retired in 1998. He could meet any challenge, from hundreds at the French Contest to a formal event in the East Parlor or Social Room.

Chestnut Hill was still a bargain in 1980 at $4,350 a year for room, board, and tuition. Even in 1983, it cost only $5,900, but the full-time traditional enrollment began to fall. These low costs had their downside. The College was perceived as one of lower quality than its more highly priced competitors. A tuition increase would help the image; but it risked lower-income students, especially in the days of rapidly mounting inflation and the declining student aid of the Reagan years.

Sister Matthew Anita was inaugurated on October 23, 1980. To her left is Dr. Mary Patterson McPherson, Bryn Mawr College, and to her right is Roseanita Schubert Coffey and John McCarthy, Board members.

This raised the question, just what is the image of Chestnut Hill? Faculty and students discussed the issue. All agreed on a small, Catholic, liberal arts college for women; some suggested co-education. No one disputed the liberal arts; small at this point was too small, and Catholic, while not rejected, needed a broader interpretation. Despite widespread changes in the seventies, some outsiders still perceived Chestnut Hill College as a convent boarding school. An appropriate logo would express tradition defined in the prism of the eighties.

Thomas Paul, Inc., became marketing consultant. They suggested more attractive publicity, a consistent image, and a new logo projecting a picture of a woman's college, open to the future, dignified yet gentle. A student's perspective is positive and imaginative: "Perhaps you think that the flowing script expresses a movement toward the future a graceful energy that propels us forward. No longer do stagnant block letters spell out *Chestnut Hill College.* The curls on the edges of each letter . . . intertwine. . . . But notice how the lines separate too, and are allowed to go their own way. Some tradition survives in the logo, as it must in the CHC community. The seal has remained; however, the circle which usually surrounded it has been removed. In fact, there are no boundaries around the entire logo. There is a definite sense of freedom expressed in this design. No box will separate

Chestnut Hill from the rest of the page just as the college itself will not be separated from the rest of the world."[55]

The marketing company noted that the College, despite its sixty years of existence, was not well known. Sister Mary Xavier had brought it into the eyes of the Chestnut Hill Community; it now had to reach a larger audience. The Admissions Office used direct mailing to students requesting it on their SAT examinations. Gradually it bore fruit. By the end of the eighties the traditional population began to climb slowly. Students came from foreign lands as yet untapped, Japan and the Pacific Rim, to the satisfaction of parents who sought a woman's college where their daughters could receive individual attention in an atmosphere of moral values.

The increase in racial, ethnic, and religious diversity corresponded to the College's mission to help women of all social classes realize their best potential, as scholars, leaders, and persons. There had always been a minority of non-Catholics and non-Christians, who welcomed the moral values of a Chestnut Hill education, and became loyal alumnae. Ethnic diversity appeared in the fifties and sixties; racial diversity, in the seventies. Previously, international students came to absorb American culture, either through exchanges, or as war refugees who planned on becoming American citizens. Minorities of the late seventies and eighties, in contrast, wanted to preserve their ethnic and racial heritage. They needed recognition for who they were, and needed to find their role in a changing American society.

The College was faced with the challenge of this dilemma. Ethnic and racial groups did not mingle. An effort at international roommates sometimes worked, but not always. The cultural differences were insurmountable for young people. Special workshops helped faculty and administration to understand differences. The Pew Grant for International Studies and Communication funded faculty workshops and the development of courses

137

with an international focus. As student leadership among minorities grew, and training sessions intensified, minority women could find their own potential and thus influence their peers. Adult learners also represented various ethnic, religious, and racial groups. They were mobile; they came for a few semesters and for family, financial, or personal reasons, dropped off. Intensive recruitment through mailings, visits to malls and businesses helped to increase the adult population. The best publicity continued to be word of mouth, from satisfied friends and relatives.

Efforts at enrollment had creative solutions. One of the most original was called "Some Leaders Are Born Women." Proposed in 1986 and implemented in 1987, the two-week summer session recruited academically motivated high school leaders. They took a three-credit college-level course and attended leadership seminars. There was no tuition charge. The students who participated returned to their schools as better leaders, already oriented to a college experience. Some chose to attend Chestnut Hill, and continued as leaders.

Two other programs addressed the young and the elderly. College for Senior Citizens has functioned since 1982. Seniors have a one-week college experience, choosing three noncredit classes. Afternoon and evening activities provide culture and fun. Many seniors choose to live on campus. Since the program varies, many satisfied customers return, often with a friend. On the other end of the spectrum are the young. The Summer Arts Camp for Children made its appearance in 1984. The six-week program consists of classes for fun and artistic enrichment. Children end the session by dramatic or musical performances, and display their artwork. Admiring parents, families, and friends come to applaud them. In this program too, many satisfied customers return, often with a sibling or a friend.

Graduate and Continuing Education numbers filled the gap in the finances and numbers left by a lower traditional enrollment. It did not solve all the problems, however, since the College for Women remained at the heart of Chestnut Hill. Its retention rate was lower but young people were also mobile. Some wanted to move away from home or closer to home; others sought a different experience. A consortium of thirteen Sisters of St. Joseph Colleges, begun in 1987, allowed students to attend any one at the cost of the home tuition. Study abroad increased.

Students went on intersessions to England, France, and Russia. The International Studies Program, begun in 1985, provided the opportunity for internships abroad since faculty could arrange them with the help of a generous Pew Foundation Grant in 1986. Students worked at the Vatican Radio, a Montessori school in Rome, an art gallery in Paris, a tourist agency in Japan, and later in Columbia, South America, and Turkey. In fact, internships became a must in many departments, for experience in the real world. Not all were to exotic lands; most were

Sister Kathryn Miller, academic dean (1980–1993) is currently administrative assistant to Sister Carol Vale.

in the immediate area. With the Communications Certificate begun in 1981 students interned at local radio and television stations. A total of eighty Science majors worked in labs and pharmaceutical companies from 1981 to 1986; they also found jobs there after graduation, often aided by College career days.

But all work and no play makes college a dull place. Student publications describe the usual dances, and a fashion show, called *Fleur de Lis*, begun in 1983. It continued until the demise in 1988 of the newspaper now named *The Fourth Estate*. Local fashion stores sponsored the event; students modeled in the Rotunda. The proceeds helped to support the paper, which featured good writing and layout. It won a second place award from the Columbia Scholastic Press Association for the 1984–1985 editions. The quality began to deteriorate as in the past, and the editors lament a scarcity of good writers.

Many activities addressed those in need and evidenced a concern for social justice. The Campus Ministry Office, inaugurated in 1985, intensified the work begun by John Carboy, SJ. A group called Mustard Seed emphasized respect for life. Members contributed articles to the newspaper; sponsored speakers on El Salvador, a clothing drive for the poor of Philadelphia, and drives for needy missions. Others participated in walks for hunger, and instituted a fast on campus. They donated the savings to the hungry. The dance-a-thon for leukemia was followed by many years of a rock-a-thon, where rocking chairs filled Fournier foyer for twenty-four hours, and heads spun as fun and charity mixed.

Peace Net, organized in 1989 by faculty, staff, and students, addressed justice issues in a peaceful and scholarly manner. Members organized cultural awareness events, including a symposium on Iran. They went to the United Nations and met international representatives. In 1992, just before the collapse of the Soviet Union, a panel focused on Soviet cultures with faculty, student, and guest-speaker participation. When the Gulf War erupted, a teach-in informed the packed audience about Arab cultures, the morality of war, and the theme of war through the ages.

If students gave social life the lowest marks, they gave the faculty the highest. They seemed pleased with academics, found the classes stimulating, and the faculty accessible and helpful. Yet they questioned the role of sisters in the dormitories. They preferred resident assistants, even if the sisters remained. The College reflected. Funds were lacking; training was needed. A limited experiment with resident assistants began in 1989, along with leadership training. Gradually RA's staffed all the residence halls, resulting in greater student responsibility.

The costs of all these undertakings pointed to the need for a Capital Campaign. The College had never engaged in one before. Undaunted, in 1986, Sister Matthew undertook a feasibility study with the consultants Marts and Lundy, Inc. Their conclusions contained some surprising observations: potential donors did not know that the College existed; alumnae were not aware of the College's needs. Yet they noted a willingness to work, a positive attitude toward the College, and the conviction that the time was

The logo chosen for the eighties is feminine and open.

Diversity is evident in this class picture (below), taken in 1989, compared to the class of 1931 (above).

Sisters Barbara Nolan, professor, and Mary Kieran, director of the program "Some Leaders Are Born Women" share the joy of the students as they receive Chestnut Hill College tee shirts.

ripe for a campaign. With the approval of the Board, the project was launched in 1988, with a goal of four million dollars and Barbara D'Iorio Martino, '60, as the dynamic and dedicated chair.

The campaign planned to improve the sports and science facilities, renovate the Cafeteria into the award winning Student Center, and increase technology. At first a new Science building looked promising, with St. Joseph's Hall becoming a Humanities Center, according to the recommendation of the Long-Range Planning Committee in 1985. The cost, however, was prohibitive. Instead, they chose to modernize the Science labs on the fifth floor of St. Joseph's Hall, virtually untouched since 1928.

The team worked quietly and quickly. Former Secretary of Transportation, Drew Lewis, delivered the keynote address for the Kickoff in March 1988. Within one year, they realized half of the goal through gifts and pledges. The implementation began at once. A new gym floor revitalized indoor sports. Within eighteen months, the pool and locker room were refurbished; a Physical Fitness Center replaced the old locker room. Faculty received salary increments, through a three-year adjustment plan. In 1991, the Technology Center opened on the ground floor of St. Joseph's Hall, formerly a recreation room dating back to the days of Mount St. Joseph Academy. The campaign was going

well. Sister Matthew's term was scheduled to end in 1990, but the Board of Directors, anxious to complete the project, extended it for another two years. Sister Matthew welcomed the opportunity, and was touched by the willingness of her administrative team to remain with her.

From 1990 to 1992, all the projects planned were completed, with the exception of the Science renovations. The Capital Campaign exceeded its $4 million goal; it raised $5.3 million. In fact, during Sister Matthew's term, gift and grant income increased 421 percent from alumnae, 89 percent from corporations, 257 percent from foundations, 113 percent from governmental sources, and 179 percent from parents and friends of the College. The Endowment Fund tripled. The Annual Golf Invitational, begun in 1983, grew by 209 percent.[56] It would be a hard act to follow.

There were many other hard acts to follow as longtime faculty retired. Sister Eva Maria Lynch, professor of Biology from 1946 to 1986, was the first woman religious to be elected a fellow by the College of Physicians of Philadelphia and a member of the National Academy of Science. Sister Ann Edward Bennis, brilliant and witty professor of English, retired in 1985 after forty years. She continued writing for the Development Office until 1993. Sister Dorothy Hennessy taught Math and Physics from 1946 to 1985, oversaw the Bookstore, and only retired from active service in the Math Center in 1998. Sister Helen Veronica

141

"College for Senior Citizens" brings these eager learners into a fun-filled learning experience.

McKenna, (1958–1990) professor of Psychology before and after her term as academic dean from 1969 to 1980, also worked as transfer credit evaluator until 1998. Sister Mary Kieran McElroy, (1962–1990) professor of Chemistry, researcher, and scholar, "retired" to the Technology Center. Sister Agnes Josephine Conway,

Members of Peace Net prepare a panel for the Gulf War Teach-in.

Members of the Schubert family, which boast of fourteen alumnae, attend the first Schubert Lecture in memory of their parents, Katherine M. and William E. Schubert.

Chaim Potok, author, was the first speaker at the Schubert Lecture Series in April 1992.

(1958–1991) professor of the Classics, and former director of sisters' studies, uses her talents to research the Fathers of the Church and in Career Services. Sister Marie Thérèse Cogan, (1948–1989) continued music lessons and her Opera Showcase almost until her death in 1996.

With tighter standards set for promotion, faculty increased their professional activities. To mention the most voluminous, David Contosta and John Lukacs published numerous books and articles. Contosta's subjects dealt with Pennsylvania and Chestnut Hill, notably *Suburb in the City: Chestnut Hill, Philadelphia, 1850–1900*. Lukacs' inimitable style and original manner of looking at history also made him a popular lecturer. In 1987 he spent a semester in his native Budapest to prepare his book, *Budapest 1900*, and, while there, was invited by the German Parliament to participate in their history conference. The book was published in New York, England, France, and Japan.

Graduates of the eighties took the example of their teachers as they too continued in scholarly careers. Medical schools, among them the University of Pennsylvania and Johns Hopkins, accepted several. The Catholic University of America and the College of William and Mary, among others,

The "caf" was transformed into the Student Life Center and is open and bright like an outdoor cafe. It was featured in *Interiors* magazine.

Barbara D'Iorio Martino, '60, was the dynamic chair of the first Capital Campaign, and the donor of largest alumna and single donor gift in 1999.

accepted candidates for Law and History. A number continued their studies for a Master's Degree, many while working. A survey done of all Science majors showed that they made up almost one-fourth of all undergraduates from 1928 to 1989. About one-fourth of this number had graduate degrees. There were 144 Doctoral Degrees, seventy-eight Medical Degrees, and thirty-one Ph.D.s.[57] While statistics indicate that girls and women are less likely to study Science than boys and men, Chestnut Hill has provided an atmosphere for women to succeed in the scientific community.[58]

With a national move toward coeducation, leaders of women's colleges made a concerted effort to publicize positive statistics. Studies done by the American Association of University Women and the Carnegie Foundation cite lack of self-esteem and self-confidence among female students in coeducational colleges. The reverse was true in women's colleges. Their graduates arc more likely to hold traditionally male-dominated and high-salaried positions and to become corporate executives, they excel in networking. More tend to marry and have children. Evidently the absence of males on campus is no deterrent.

There were more positive attitudes toward women's colleges throughout the country, with applicants up 8 percent, though not yet at Chestnut Hill. Student editorials emphasize women's rights without favoring coeducation. A 1982 article notes the changing image of women's colleges. The author states that education in a woman's college is not only equal to coeducation; it often surpasses it. She adds that women who aspire to nontraditional top positions have excellent role models at Chestnut Hill College. She is proud that Chestnut Hill has chosen to remain a woman's college, and hopes to keep it that way.

A touching tribute to the self-confidence instilled at Chestnut Hill is a letter to the College in *Kaleidoscope* 1981, signed "A Well Regarding senior." She states: "Since my first day with you, you made me feel as if I really belonged. You were right—I can't imagine having gone anywhere else. You have always treated me with love, respect, understanding, whether I always happened to deserve it or not. . . . You recognized the child in me as well as the young woman. . . . I know what I am graduating from, but I don't know what I'm graduating to. I have no way of knowing what lies ahead of me, but whatever it may be seems easier to face knowing that you arc behind me." The writer was Regina Ferris, who was killed in an accident the summer after her graduation.

The year 1984 was a milestone in the annals of the College, its sixtieth anniversary. Less dramatic than the Golden Jubilee, it was nevertheless a happy occasion. Cardinal Krol celebrated the Liturgy on September 9, followed by a reception in the Rotunda. On October 3, Pulitzer Prize Winner Charles Fuller spoke about his popular play, *A Soldier's Story*. He was later

The science facilities on the fifth floor of St. Joseph's Hall were virtually untouched until the renovation of 1992. This is before and after.

graduation speaker and honorary degree recipient. Other events included "Facet of Topaz," an alumnae social; the DiPasquale String Quartet; and finally on May 1, 1985, the closing event, a lecture and reading by Irish poet and later Nobel Prize winner Seamus Heaney. Lester Conner, an annual lecturer and former director of the Yeats School in Ireland, negotiated his visit. Heaney returned in 1986 for an honorary degree. This lecture and others were sponsored by a generous grant from the Hunt Foundation.

Satisfied customers give the best publicity for Chestnut Hill College. Sister Matthew Anita worked hard to make more and more of them, especially among faculty and staff. She did not win all, by her own admission, but she made every effort. As early as 1982, she established a Staff Committee. Sister Kathryn Miller began the Faculty Colloquium Series in 1983, providing opportunities for academic enrichment. In 1986 the Pew Grant helped support faculty retreats, released time, and

opportunities for professional conferences. There was a salary raise every year, even in hard times. Sister Matthew announced publicly that no tenured professor nor any existing major would be eliminated. All administrative and staff offices were computerized by 1985. Sister Matthew joined in the mobility of the decade by frequent off-campus travels for fund-raising, board meetings of other institutions, and committee duties. Yet she was always ready to listen to anyone's concerns. She attended as many College activities as humanly possible, and personally complimented the organizers, faculty, staff, or students. When commencements came, she knew the graduating class well from her own personal involvement with them, and touchingly alluded to many events.

Sister Matthew knew the importance of positive interaction with the members of the Board and influential friends of the College. Realizing her need for expert advice, she formed the President's Council from knowledgeable and willing business people and professionals. They helped her with marketing and fund-raising techniques. She wanted more committed lay people on the Board of Directors. As valuable as the sister members were, financial expertise was equally important. In addition, Vatican II stressed collaboration with the laity, and fostered lay leadership wherever possible. By the end of her term in 1992, she set the goal of one-third religious and two-thirds lay membership. It was met within one year. The nineties have shown that the policy, as well as the choice of Board members, has brought tremendous financial and professional benefit to the College.

In 1990 *Money* magazine recognized Chestnut Hill as one of "Ten Top Values for Women," the only women's college in Pennsylvania to attain this distinction. Among the one hundred "Best College Buys" it ranked fifth in the nation's women's colleges, third among all Pennsylvania's colleges and universities, and twenty-fifth among all private colleges and universities in the

The annual Golf Invitational with Chairman Bill Magarity (second from left) was always a great success.

Northeast Region. This honor remained throughout the nineties. In 1991, *Barron's Best Buys in College Education* selected Chestnut Hill as one of three hundred nationwide institutions that has consistently provided quality education at costs below the national average. This too helped to launch the College into the new decade.

As the end of the century was in sight with the calendar turning to its last decade, the College had done more than weather the storms that had menaced it. It had defined its image in terms that harkened to the past and pointed to the future. The Middle States Report of 1991 emphasized a college for women in the nineties, cultural diversity for citizenship in a global community, and continued development of the teaching-learning process.[59] It was a time for cautious optimism. Numbers were growing, but not fast enough; the campus was getting a new look, but the aging Mount needed more help; faculty were of high professional quality, but they needed better salaries and funding for professional activities. In the thirties Sister Maria Kostka and Mother Mary James sought gifts from benefactors and especially the alumnae. Sister Catharine Frances and Sister Mary Xavier did likewise. The eighties saw a concerted effort to move to a broader base for funding. It would only become more important in the nineties, as the rhythm of life accelerated, rushing to the new millennium.

145

**The African-American Awareness Group sponsors a Fashion Show.
Nicole Jenkins displays the fashions of 1994.**

CHAPTER TWELVE
ACCELERATION

This was the information age. Faxes, e-mail, the internet erupted in the nineties. Never had life moved so quickly, or more slowly as a growing bureaucracy enmeshed all corporations, large and small, in a maze of channels. The legal system fell prey to common lawsuits; crime was on the increase; privacy was threatened as access to confidential matters was simple on the internet. Terrorism was an ever-present threat; computer technology directed wars. Chestnut Hill follows the movement of the times; sometimes spared as when student numbers grew as the economy declined during the Depression, or when the revolts of the sixties simply grazed the College; there were no Kent State tragedies here. Yet the acceleration of the nineties was hard to escape.

Sister Matthew Anita knew that a successor would be named in 1992. In her last two years she implemented the Graduate Program in Technology in Education, completed the Middle States Ten Year Accreditation Review, opened the Computer Center on the ground floor of St. Joseph's Hall, presided at the dedication of the completed Science Wing in April of 1992. The Connelly Foundation funded the Molecular Biology laboratory in memory of Bernice F. Labinski Hilinski, '44. One unforeseen project occurred at the end of her administration. It was to have a strong impact on the College.

Allentown College of St. Francis had a successful program, ACCESS, featuring continuous eight-week sessions, evenings and week-ends. It targeted working adults who had not completed a college degree. A streamlined curriculum, while based in the liberal arts, focused on majors such as Business and Human Services. Allentown already had three sites, and wanted another within a radius of Chestnut Hill. They proposed a collaborative program, whereby students could attend the Chestnut Hill campus while receiv-

Sister Matthew Anita MacDonald leaves a College ready to meet the end of the twentieth century.

ing an Allentown College degree. Both sides negotiated quickly, agreed on appropriate financial arrangements, and set the program in place for the fall of 1992. Before Sister Matthew signed the agreement with Allentown College in June of 1992, her successor had already been named.

The process was like the previous one, but began in the fall of 1991, to allow the president-elect to intern with Sister Matthew as well as at other institutions. All eligible Sisters of St. Joseph were invited to apply. At a time when many Catholic colleges had no willing or qualified religious to serve, Chestnut Hill was fortunate to have six: Sisters Helen Burke, Honor Kierans, Mary Helen Kashuba, Rosemary Scheirer, Carol Jean Vale, and Carol Zinn. They interviewed with the Search Committee and attended faculty, staff, student, and alumnae gatherings. Each candidate spoke publicly on her vision for the future of Chestnut Hill. All were well qualified, leaders in their own fields, and had a vision in harmony with the tradition and goals of the College.

On December 9, 1991, the College community waited in anticipation as the Board pondered their decision: who will lead the College into the next millennium? The choice fell upon Sister Carol Jean Vale, chair of Religious Studies and a respected scholar and theologian. She came to the College in

Sister Carol Jean Vale is named sixth president of the College on December 9, 1991.

1988 and, foreseeing the acceleration of the nineties and perhaps intuitively knowing that her teaching career would take a rapid turn, completed her dissertation and instituted the graduate degree in Holistic Spirituality and Spiritual Direction by 1990. Born in Washington, D.C., but following her marine lieutenant (later colonel) father around the country, she experienced diversity early on. Sister Carol was the first president to convert to Catholicism, which she embraced as a high school senior. After a year at St. Joseph's College in Emmitsburg, Maryland, she entered the Sisters of St. Joseph and completed her B.A. in English while teaching in various Catholic schools. She had worked in high school administration before completing her doctorate in Historical Theology at Fordham University, the first non-University of Pennsylvania graduate to become president.

Sister Carol, a person of dynamism and action, is a woman of vision in the tradition of Sister Maria Kostka. Inspired by Teilhard de Chardin, her dissertation subject and an inspiration in her vision for the College, she thinks positively. Like most of her predecessors, she was trained in English. She moves quickly; acceleration is the hallmark of her administration. Changes

happen overnight. At a lecture prior to her inauguration, John Lukacs described her as a "welcome hurricane that had blown through the halls of the College." She dreams on a grandiose scale, and gets grandiose results.

A woman with a global perspective, Sister Carol sought to bring the world to Chestnut Hill and Chestnut Hill to the world. She sought to create global leaders among the graduates. She wanted to see Chestnut Hill become a global leader in women's education. She believed in diversity, and the ability to deal with it. Committed to the Catholic identity of the College, she stated, "We don't have to apologize for our belief in God and in our Catholic heritage. . . . At [Chestnut Hill College] we know what we stand for, and we're going to continue to stand for it."[60]

She announced these goals informally before assuming office and, once again, at an elegant Investiture ceremony on October 23, 1992. Over five hundred guests attended the ninety-minute ceremony. A letter from Barbara Bush expressed congratulations from President Bush and herself. Alumnae, student, and church leaders gave greetings. Anita M. Pampusch, Ph.D., president of the College of St. Catherine in St. Paul, gave the keynote address.

Finally, in an eloquent Inaugural Address, acclaimed as one of the finest, the new president cited the traditions of the College and the goals of her administration. She stressed the globalization of the human community and Chestnut Hill's role in attaining it; the importance of women in today's world: "Women working together can change the face of nations. Is it not time for women's voices to be heard and heeded, for women's leadership styles to be implemented and imitated?" She emphasized her confidence in the power of the College: "It is my firm belief that Chestnut Hill College can be a positive power of transformation in the world in which we live. To this end, we strive to educate not just global citizens, worthy as that goal may be, but global leaders."

148

The celebration continued with food and feasting for all members of the College community, from a champagne reception in the Rotunda to a special dinner for students. Drs. Lukacs and Contosta presented "Neighbors, Past and Present," with special emphasis on Chestnut Hill. Logue Library had an exhibit on College history. The campus was alive with joy and hope.

Reality soon succeeded celebration. Although the earlier Capital Campaign had brought in many contributions, needs soon outstripped resources, and not all pledges materialized. The historic buildings needed attention: repairs in the physical plant, refurnishing of many faded areas, transformation of underused space into areas for more immediate needs. Offices moved to more adequate locations where dormitory space was no longer needed. The President's Office, having long outgrown the small space in Fournier Hall, moved to the former faculty room on the second floor of St. Joseph's Hall. The Social Room, last redecorated in the fifties, got a brighter look. The East Parlor was redone with scenes of Philadelphia. The student lounges in Fontbonne, untouched since 1962, were redecked. Much of this took place at the speed of light in this age of acceleration.

Other initiatives, a consortium with neighboring colleges to implement a telecommunications network, a nationwide search for a dean of the College, and a comprehensive physical plant needs assessment, followed immediately. In 1992 the newly formed Long-Range Planning Committee involved every member of the College community and many alumnae in large and small group discussions. A new curriculum, global orientation, priority for women's education, greater diversity, and a new image were their top priorities. Service Master, the newly hired campus maintenance supervision firm, was commissioned for a facilities study.

Meanwhile, 1993 brought a somber side to the optimism of the new administration. There was a deficit of

Mayor Edward J. Rendell is robed for the Inauguration Ceremony where he will congratulate President Carol Vale in the name of the city on October 23, 1992.

Newly inaugurated President Carol Jean Vale (center) joins Sister Margaret Fleming, chair of the Board of Directors (left), and Sister Kathryn Miller, academic dean.

Trumpeters herald the Inaugural Procession.
Photo courtesy of Larry Salese Photography, Inc.

$100,000; enrollment was falling. To add to the problems, the harsh winter saw sixteen storms in ten weeks; bushes and trees were harmed or destroyed; pipes burst in the newly renovated Science Center; flooding eroded road surfaces; floors buckled. Resources were limited and needs were immediate. Stephen Lightcap, a professional

149

CFO, joined the staff in 1994 and ordered a budget freeze.

Yet progress continued. The College was ranked for the fourth consecutive year in *Money* magazine as the "Top 100 best buys" and was seventh among the top ten women's colleges. Women's colleges gained in prestige as TV shows such as "20/20," "Sixty Minutes," "Oprah Winfrey," "Dateline NBC" emphasized their importance. New majors emerged, including a B.S. in Environmental Science. The Graduate Program planned additional Master's Degrees and a Doctoral Program. The Core Curriculum proposed Philadelphia as a focus for a first-year core course. Gifts continued: a scholarship by Nancy O'Shea Devlin, '64, another from Rohm and Haas, and an anonymous donation of $40,000. The Southeastern Pennslyvania Consortium for Higher Education received $2 million for the development of technology. The Spirituality Program received a grant of $39,000; the Mandell Foundation gave $25,000 for a CD Rom in the Library; an energy grant from Pennsylvania brought $23,000, and the Luciano Tuition Scholarship of $135,000 helped the situation. Yet money was not the only challenge.

Obviously a new image was imperative. Without denying tradition, the College needed to risk a renewed identity as it moved into the third millennium. It now had three distinct divisions: the rapidly growing Graduate Division, ACCESS, soon to be transformed into ACCELERATED, and the traditional College for Women. A more diverse population comprised this oldest segment of the College community. Women who needed various support systems, single mothers, the economically and academically disadvantaged, lived side by side with a more traditional clientele. They all had potential; Chestnut Hill could give them the opportunity to become competent women leaders.

In the age of telemarketing, outside help was imperative. Mark Thompson Associates began a Master Space Study Plan and Schultz and Williams ad-

Philadelphia greets the new president.

Mayor Rendell greets Bridget McGovern, class president, as first-year students use Philadelphia as the basis of their core course.

A new image for the nineties is found in this logo.

dressed marketing. Their conclusions were innovative and optimistic: renew and refresh the image of the College; modernize the facilities and, above all, plan for a new building. This had been the unrealized hope of the previous administration. Here again Sister Carol fulfilled the mandate for fund-raising given her on her appointment.

Among the goals for the College was increased enrollment. In the sixties, there were 298 colleges for women; by 1998, only seventy-nine. Like all other colleges, Chestnut Hill suffered from the economic crunch, demographic changes, the uncertainty of federal funding, the challenge to nonprofit schools, and fewer grants. Admissions planned newer strategies, and under the direction of Schulz and Williams, inaugurated the Success Kit for the College for Women, focusing on successful alumnae. An updated recruitment video stressed success, a warm and caring atmosphere, and academic excellence. Radio, billboard, newspaper, and television advertising emphasized the convenient accessible location, beautiful and stimulating neighborhood community, small classes, and an attractive, safe campus. Additional committed recruiters joined the staff. Reverend Eugene Kole, dean of the Graduate Division, assumed the role of enrollment manager until his appointment as president of Quincy College in 1997. Kathleen Rex Anderson, dean of ACCELERATED, continued his work.

The marketing study demonstrated that the logo of the eighties, very feminine and open, did not capture the reality of the nineties. The three divisions of the College needed adequate representation. Thus a new graphic identity was professionally designed. It was clear, direct, and appropriate to the mission of the College. It could address a diverse audience, which the College sought to attract through its three divisions. Red and white gradually replaced the original brown and gold and added luster to banners around the campus and to new sports uniforms.

The marketing consultants and most of the College community believed in the feasibility of a College for Women. Their confidence and the direct marketing techniques produced dividends in the late nineties. Enrollment rose; the quality of students improved, and the spirit of the College remained alive. Fortunately, the growing numbers in the other two divisions helped the College for Women, and contented customers, always the best source of recruitment, supported all three divisions.

Continuing Education, addressed primarily to women beyond traditional

college age, did not grow as hoped. Merged with the College for Women, it had possibilities. In November of 1995, Sister Carol proposed a special designation for these women. They would become Kirby students, in honor of Sister Mary Xavier Kirby who initiated the program in 1969.

Traditional students in the nineties

Sister Carol Vale (left) congratulates Sister Mary Xavier Kirby at the Inauguration of the Kirby Program for Nontraditional Women.

A scholarship for Kirby students was instituted in memory of Sister Catherine McDonald, former director of Continuing Education, and deceased in 1997.

are also in a mode of acceleration. They must work to meet rising costs; they need to graduate quickly, sometimes in less than four years. As the nineties evolved, their comings and goings were frequent, and they requested increased campus security, improved through the efforts of Jim Hansen. Contrary to the students of the seventies who clamored for permission to smoke in their rooms and in most public places, the nineties sought a smoke-free campus. Although most found no problem with an all-women's college, they wanted male visitation in the dorms, begun in 1992, with weekend extensions in 1996 after a well-organized student poll.

Student publications are often a vehicle for such issues and concerns. A newspaper returned in 1995, called *CHC Voices*, and has expanded into three or four issues a year. It contains reflective editorials, positive statements on student activities, and suggestions for improvements on campus. *The Grackle* had ceased to exist in the six-

ties. No literary publication replaced it, despite some short-lived efforts. In 1996 *Sketches from the Hill* restored a creative focus to college writing. The first issues contained mainly poetry; later they expanded into short stories, mainly dealing with issues of the nineties: teenage pregnancy, race relations, religious doubt, terminal cancer. The publication improved in quantity and quality, and has survived up to Volume IV, while still not rivaling Mithridates.

Career awareness is the focus of many programs. Among the most innovative is a program called "Career Connections." Students choose an alumna working in a field that interests them. After careful selection and an orientation, the student then con-

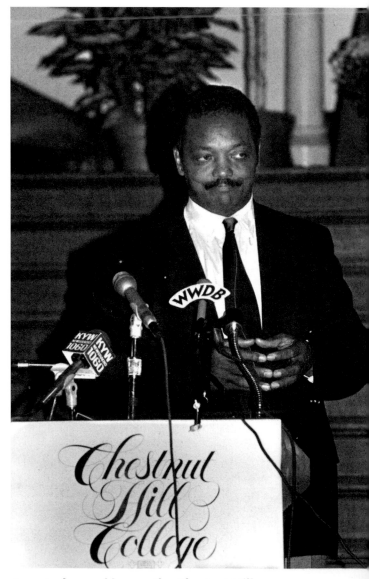

Jesse Jackson addresses the Chestnut Hill community on September 14, 1992.

Jessica Wormley, '97, receives an award as one of twenty-five Women of Justice.

The lacrosse team in 1998 boasts of a long history of success.

tacts the alumna and arranges a shadow visit to the site of employment. The program seeks to help the student explore a career in a realistic workplace setting, to demonstrate the value of a college education, and to foster early contact between alumnae and students. Since 1994, it has produced positive results on both sides. It often leads the student to a career she may never have considered, and encourages lasting contacts.

Under the direction of Patricia McGlynn, '54, director of Career Services, the College has sponsored a Job Fair in March since 1990. Since 1995, the College has participated in the Teacher Job Fair, held at a local convention center. Representatives from over 125 school districts throughout the country attend, and over two thousand students from the area come to seek employment. Since Education heads the majors at the College in the late nineties, the Fair addresses the needs of many graduates. In this age of acceleration, it is not unusual to find career changes three and four times in a person's working lifetime. These programs open the undergraduate's mind

Dr. Alma Dea Morani, plastic surgeon, later donated an impressive mask collection to the College.

Sister Helen Prejean, author of *Dead Man Walking*, addresses the graduating class of 1996.

John Lukacs and Mario Vargas Llora are Ingersoll Prize Winners in 1992.

to several options.

Like their sisters in the eighties, students of the nineties still insist that life on campus is dull. The dean of Student Life and her assistants, along with Student Government representatives, have initiated many activities, among them: make your own video, the roommate game, Reading outlet trip, and a multicultural show. Yet the student population of the nineties is diverse in age, ethnicity, race, and religion. One group's idea of entertainment or service is not necessarily universal. The nineties saw new clubs: Hispanics in Action, the African American and the Asian American Awareness Groups. At first limited to specific ethnic groups, they are slowly involving other segments of the student population. On the whole, student life has gradually evolved away from the campus, mainly because of changing times and conditions, and the nineties present a very different focus from the early days. Yet in many ways they are similar.

Miriam Flaherty Quinn, '36, had noted that a social conscience was necessary then as now. Throughout the years, students have addressed social justice. In the nineties, Campus Ministry has fostered help to the needy, Good Works to economically deprived areas, Students for Peace and Justice, and intercollegiate retreats. Walks for AIDS victims, work in soup kitchens, and ten years of fund-raising for People Making Progress are only a few avenues of social concern. Jessica Wormley, '97, was honored by *Network*

as one of twenty-five "Women of Justice," the only undergraduate in the group. She and three others spent their winter break in the Otomi Indian Village in San Pedro Martir, Mexico, where they built brick walls, flattened roads, and helped Indian children. They raised the money for the trip themselves, and quietly helped those in need, faithful to the mission and tradition of the College.

The Sports Program is growing in size and importance. The new building will contain a larger gym with spectator space, and the recruitment of athletes is a growing priority. Early in the nineties, renovations in the pool permitted swimming for adults and children, adult water aerobics, scuba diving, lifeguard training and water safety. Under the capable direction of Lorraine Busch and Janice Kuklick, who succeeded the devoted "Miss B," athletes have returned early for training since 1991. As a result, the teams received many awards in the nineties: Volleyball Division IV Invitational Second Place in 1990–1991, and PAIAW Runner-up in 1996–1997; tennis awards from 1992 to 1995, the last being PAIAW Champion, with the same award for softball in 1996–1997. Lacrosse holds the highest record, not surprising, since the dynamic Janice Kuklick herself was PAIAW Coach of the Year in 1986–1987, 1991–1992, and tied in 1997–1998. The Lacrosse teams were consistent PAIAW Champions from 1978-1993. Yet the spirit of sports at Chestnut Hill remained the same; all were welcome, beginners and advanced, and although victory is good, fair play and improvement are better, as articulated in the CHC Athletic Philosophy.

The College continued to provide notable lecturers for the enrichment of both students and faculty. A series of lectures on cancer research, organized in 1993 through the efforts of Lakshmi Atchison, featured eminent scholars in the field, who donate their services to the project. Other nationally known figures, such as Jesse Jackson in October of 1992; Jill Ker Conway, through the Schubert Lecture in 1995; Sister Helen Prejean; Christopher Matthews; Cokie Roberts; and Mary Higgins Clark have come to campus. In October of 1996, Monika Hellwig, formerly professor of Theology at Georgetown and executive director of the Association of Catholic Colleges and Universities, gave the keynote address for a workshop on the mission of the College, then in the process of revision.

On February 14, 1994, a celebration honored the retirement of seven sisters whose cumulative service totaled more than three hundred years. The College established the Chestnut Hill College Scholarship for Leadership and Academic Excellence in honor of the Sisters of St. Joseph. The honorees were Sisters Consuelo Maria Aherne, Ann Edward Bennis, Agnes Josephine Conway, Mary Julia Daly, Rita Madeleine Gruber, Mary Jordan, and Eva Maria Lynch. The scholarship had generated $34,000 in 1994; these were well-loved professors.

The year 1994 also brought the retirement of another familiar face on campus since 1947, Professor John Lukacs. Renowned as one of the great historians of the twentieth century, he is the author of fifteen books and literally hundreds of articles. He considered *Historical Consciousness* as his most important work and tried to instill critical thinking into his students. Perhaps the greatest tribute was his presence on campus. David Contosta observes: "Just knowing that he was there conveyed a sense of belonging to a wider community of scholars that enveloped the college and spilled out into the world, far beyond our small beacon on the hill."

Another loss came with the retirement in 1995 of Josephine Albarelli, professor of Spanish for almost fifty years. She inspired love of literature and culture in all who knew her. A connoisseur of art, she collected remarkable Mexican works. Students and colleagues frequently came to her home on the Parkway, and shared her breadth of culture. Very involved in the

Dr. Lakshmi Atchison organized a Biomedical Seminar featuring prominent speakers such as Carlo M. Croce, M.D., director of the Jefferson Cancer Institute and Center, who was opening speaker in 1994.

College, she championed consultation with administration whenever possible. Her insights were perceptive and original, and a conversation or a meeting with her was sure to produce a new idea.

For several years faculty had shared in decision-making through Faculty Concerns and various committees. Negotiations for a Faculty Senate began in 1992 between representatives from faculty and administration. The first formal collaboration occurred in 1994, when both groups met to find a new dean of the College. After 1995, the Senate assumed greater independence. All full-time faculty were members, and an elected Executive Board prepared the agenda. The Senate is a forum where faculty can discuss issues among themselves and communicate with the administration.

Faculty at this time needed redistribution of forces. The administration of small departments was costly and sometimes time consuming. A solution was not easy. In 1995 a divisional structure replaced the complex departmental organization. Divisional heads led Natural Sciences, Social Sciences, Humanities, Education, and Technology and Business, in the hope of encouraging a more interdisciplinary approach to learning. The system had merits: faculty could teach, unencumbered by administrative duties. Budget pooling permitted greater flexibility. Money could be economized by limiting the released time given to former department chairs. It also had its negative side. Some faculty felt they were not consulted sufficiently about the change and refused to support it. Divisional heads were not always familiar with the former departments, which were left with advising and planning in addition to a fuller teaching schedule. Faculty debated the merits of the new system for two years, until it was re-evaluated in 1997. Sister Carol, who moves quickly, is also willing to reassess quickly. Discussions ensued, proposals came to the floor, and eventually a vote overwhelmingly favored a return to the departmental system,

Students from Holy Spirit Junior College in Nagoya, Japan, who come regularly for a summer program, pose here in 1987.

Host families receive the Japanese students for weekends. Constance McCarthy Boylan poses here with her son and her two guests.

which began implementation in 1998–1999.

Another major challenge was the reorganization of administration to permit greater articulation within the College community and with the broader academic world. In 1992, the chief development officer (executive director of Institutional Advancement) became part of the administration. Gradually vice-presidential offices were created and by 1999 the system was composed of vice-presidents of Academic Affairs

(William Walker), Financial Affairs (Elizabeth Kroger), Student Affairs (Rosemary Scheirer, SSJ), and Institutional Advancement (Lorraine Aurely). The number of deans also increased to meet the growing needs in ACCELERATED, Graduate, and the College for Women.

Although almost fifty sisters continue to serve the College, their number has decreased. Vatican II had emphasized the empowerment of the laity. Previously only Sisters of St. Joseph composed the administration; now it included both lay and religious. The Board of Directors was now two-thirds lay people. Lay professors and staff outnumbered religious by far. One problem was financial; sisters received far less compensation; additional funds were needed. The Strategic Plan makes salaries one of the main priorities and the president's success in fund-raising lends optimism to the challenge.

Another aspect was philosophical: the mission of the College was deeply rooted in the charism of the Sisters of St. Joseph; would it remain with a diverse population? Yet the new mission statement, approved by the Board in December of 1997, has become familiar to the College community. It focuses on the original spirit, academic excellence, links between the worlds of work and learning, values and beliefs, and local and global connections. It still harks back to the 1924 mission statement: "to give opportunity to young women desirous of a college education in an atmosphere of religion and culture."

Academically faculty remain involved and innovative. New undergraduate majors appeared: Communication and Technology, Fine Arts, and Technology in 1993; Environmental Science in 1994; and Applied Technology in 1997. Minors reappeared, and are popular among students. The Core Curriculum, approved for implementation in the fall of 1999, stresses critical thinking, technological literacy, communication skills, and interdisciplinary learning. Students commend accessible, friendly,

and helpful teachers. The Marketing Analysis by Schulz and Williams shows that more than 89 percent of the students interviewed were very satisfied with academics.[61] A caring and competent faculty is among CHC's best assets.

Faculty are involved beyond the classroom. They are active in research and publishing. Books include David Contosta's *The History of Villanova University* and Joseph Micucci's *The Adolescent in Family Therapy: Breaking the Cycle of Conflict and Control*, Sister Cecelia Cavanaugh's *The Drawings of Lorca*. Articles in professional journals are too numerous to mention.[62] Professors present their research at scholarly meetings, both nationally and internationally. Faculty have taught in other institutions, including Sisters Rita Michael Scully and Marganne Drago at Holy Spirit Junior College in Nagoya, Japan. They have received honors from prominent associations, such as *Palmes Académiques* and the Association for Women in Science. With faculty help departments have organized special programs, such as the Symposium for the tercentenary of Sor Juana Ines de la Cruz and the centenary of Lorca's and Alexandre's birth, both prepared by Sister Cecelia Cavanaugh. Sister Carol Vale gives the example of scholarship to her colleagues, with numerous presentations and several theological articles.

The nineties have been the space age for Chestnut Hill. Early alumnae return looking for the Arcade, demolished in 1984; alumnae of the eighties will not be able to find the dean's or president's office, and will instead stumble upon ACCELERATED. If they look for their comfortable rooms on the third floor of St. Joseph's Hall, they will find offices. Career Services has taken over what used to be St. Joseph's Chapel, and the Infirmary houses the dean and the vice-president for Academic Affairs. Tiffany Lounge, or the "Day Hop" has become offices. Those who suffered through the summer heat can breathe more easily in the air-conditioned spaces of the second and fifth floors of St. Joseph's Hall. Alumnae are delighted to use an inviting terrace outside Fournier, which in good weather becomes an outdoor café. The outdoors meets the indoors through glass doors along the front corridor of Fournier. The chapel which Mother Mary Louis Murphy wanted all to pass, but not to pass by, meets the passer-by also through glass. Although the roofs may look the same, they have been entirely replaced and should last for another seventy-five years.

The renovations of these faded areas are very costly. Sister Carol Jean Vale, building on the hard work of her predecessors, is the finest fund-raiser the College has ever had. She has traveled far and wide to interest alumnae in future projects. She initiated a four-phase forty million dollar Capital Gifts Initiative, and worked tirelessly to interest donors. The Connelly Foundation contributed an initial $2.5 million on April 6, 1998, the largest gift in the College's history. Ann Rusnack Sorgenti, '58, contributed $1 million dollars on January 28, 1998; an anonymous donor another million, and a third came from the estate of Rita M. Tofini, '38. New Year's Eve of 1998 brought another million from a previous donor. The Board of Directors, including alumnae, has pledged over $6 million. Alumnae, including Board members, have pledged over $6.3 million. On April 8, 1999, devoted alumna Barbara D'Iorio Martino, '60, along with her husband Rocco, presented the largest alumna and single donor gift of $2.5 million. With such success, perhaps the Initiative may not need the thirty-five years planned.

Under the leadership of Sister Carol Jean Vale the enrollment in the three Divisions of the College has grown from 1,235 in the spring of 1992 to 1,784 in the spring of 1999. The endowment has doubled, as has annual giving, reaching an all time high of $501,000. The Capital Gifts Initiative has raised an unprecedented $11,445,000 from only sixty-four donors. The College now looks forward to its first new building

in almost forty years. To be known as the Barbara Martino Hall, it will include convocation and athletic facilities, a Communication and Technology Center.

Sister Mary Xavier made the College known to the Chestnut Hill Community, Sister Matthew Anita increased visibility locally, city- and statewide; Sister Carol has entered the national arena. She is a member of national boards, and has given keynote addresses and papers throughout the country. She has entered into collaborative agreements with neighboring institutions. During her tenure, the world has come to the College through the development of technology. Logue Library has been brought on-line and completely automated. Faculty will soon have access to the Internet in their offices and students in their rooms.

In only seven years, Sister Carol has more than fulfilled the mandate she accepted at her inauguration. She has furthered academic excellence through new graduate and undergraduate programs, the ACCELERATED Division, and student and faculty accomplishments. She has created a vibrant, committed, and enthusiastic Board of Directors. Yet she is a person who listens, who smiles, who brings elegance and eloquence to every event. She observes, "As Chestnut Hill College moves into the twenty-first century there is every reason for optimism and celebration. This past year has been historic in multiple ways and the future may hold ever finer moments."

Sister Carol Jean Vale, Maria Mandell, Ann Rusnack Sorgenti, and Sister Margaret Fleming look to the future. Ann was the first alumna donor of one million dollars.

Sister Carol Jean Vale contemplates the future
as she stands in historic St. Joseph's Hall.

St. Joseph's Hall keeps the name of Mount Saint Joseph Collegiate Institute.

The tower of the Convent Chapel, scene of many College formal events, rises above the spring foliage.

The Lourdes Grotto was the scene of May Day crownings, and remains a favorite spot for the College community and visitors.

Students enjoy the spring sun on the flowering campus.

 The Summer House, located near the Grotto and the House of Loreto, is a welcome spot for outdoor events. *Photo courtesy of Miriam R. Allorto*

Fournier Hall is visible in the distance as the drive winds around St. Joseph's Hall.

Fournier Hall and the Library enclose the Circle at the end of the winding drive into the College.

Students picnic on the lawn in good weather.

The arches in front of St. Joseph's Hall welcome the visitor.

St. Joseph's Hall was the first home of Mount Saint Joseph College, and continues to be a focal point of the campus. *Photo courtesy of Miriam R. Allorto*

Fournier Hall, built in 1928, sparkles with the new roofs it received in 1998–1999.

The Investiture Ceremony takes place in the Chapel during Family Weekend.

The Procession wends its way along campus paths at Commencement.

Students welcome winter snows, which might mean a holiday from classes and outdoor winter fun.

New computer labs equip the College for both graduate and undergraduate programs in Technology.

CHAPTER THIRTEEN
XIII
EXPANSION

In 1999 few colleges can consider themselves exclusively women's liberal arts colleges; there are different educational needs today. People who left high school for a career ten, twenty years ago, suddenly find that there is no advancement for them. The younger graduate, armed with a Bachelor's Degree, takes their intended job. They too must get a degree. Yet they cannot stop work and return to college. In fact, the carefree life of a college student no longer attracts them, but the degree does. Chestnut Hill heard their voices and responded with ACCESS in collaboration with Allentown College in 1992.

Numbers came at first. ACCESS was open to both men and women.

They filled the first floor of Clement Hall in the evenings until 10:30 p.m., Mondays through Thursdays. These students-by-night and salaried professionals-by-day sought an Allentown College degree, and were little involved with Chestnut Hill. Yet as time went on, they hardly knew Allentown College, and began to consider themselves members of the Chestnut Hill College community. Publicity and recruitment were confusing. Their numbers also dwindled, since the marketing addressed almost exclusively African American women. The Philadelphia urban population did not respond to the Allentown marketing. Allentown College considered closing the site. In the summer of 1995, both colleges agreed that it would be of mutual benefit to transfer the program to Chestnut Hill College. Technical questions, especially financial aid,

Dr. Kathleen Rex Anderson (center), director of ACCELERATED, smiles with satisfaction with the first graduating class in 1996.

ACCELERATED gives more than a B.S.; it gave Mr. and Mrs. to graduates Bruce Johnson and Mary Stitt, in September 1998.

delayed the actual implementation until January 1996. The new division was called *ACCELERATED*. Kathleen Rex Anderson, '66, assumed the role of dean.

While ACCESS languished, ACCELERATED grew. In the first semester alone, it increased by 240 percent. Kathleeen Anderson led a marketing campaign that targeted various segments of the population. Attractive radio and TV ads highlighted a beautiful and safe campus, convenient to the city and the suburbs, accessible by public transportation, a caring and competent faculty, and excellent instruction. By 1999, the program enrolled 30 percent males. The racial composition was 45 percent white; 55 percent African American and other minorities.

ACCELERATED features six eight-week sessions throughout the year. Students may come in the evenings, early mornings, or on Saturdays. They may submit transfer credits, portfolio assessments, or challenge examinations to accelerate their studies even further. Each individual follows a different path; some study every session; some miss one or two. Some prefer the weekend; others choose evenings. Flexibility characterizes the program. There are ten majors: Accounting and Business, Business Communications

(the fastest growing), Computer Science, Criminal Justice, Dependent Care Management, Human Resources Management, Human Services, Management (the two largest), Marketing, and Social Gerontology. Students may apply for a certificate, an Associate Degree, or a Bachelor's Degree.

Since convenience is vital, courses are offered not only on campus, but at Einstein Hospital and the Police Academy. A mobile population needs help reaching its destinations. While the alternate sites cut down on travel time, the beauty and friendliness of the main campus provides an inspiring atmosphere for learning. Besides, the friendly faces that meet these people are what often endears them most to the College. The best marketing for any program has always been by word of mouth.

ACCELERATED is still developing. Although it follows the guidelines for a liberal arts education, it differs from the traditional CHC curriculum, yet awards the same degree. This caused faculty concern. They requested greater participation in course planning and hiring; many took advantage of this opportunity. Full-time faculty of the College for Women are impressed with the diligence and motivation of the

Sister Carol Jean Vale joins Police Commissioner John Timoney as an agreement is reached for an alternate ACCELERATED site.

Edward Ashburn is proud of his scholarship to ACCELERATED, awarded to the Police Academy on July 31, 1998.

Reverend Daniel G. Gambet, OSFS, and Carol Jean Vale, SSJ, sign an agreement to offer CHC's masters in Counseling Psychology at Allentown College on March 9, 1995.

ACCELERATED students. On the whole, they are equal to and sometimes superior to the traditional student. They work hard, since their careers depend on this degree.

Plans are already in process for an M.S. in Human Service Administration that will follow an accelerated format. New majors in Child Care and Health Care Management are being explored. Alternate sites, such as the local community colleges and local corporate sites may be added. ACCELERATED plans collaboration with other existing programs, such as Paralegal Studies. Students and graduates continue to recommend the program to their friends and colleagues. As with all of Chestnut Hill's projects, personal contact is the best advertising. Satisfied customers bring many more to campus. ACCELERATED students spontaneously praise a flexible schedule, personal attention, devoted and competent faculty, and a degree of excellence.

If ACCELERATED has been the hare of the traditional fable, the Graduate Program has been the tortoise. As early as 1977, the College had begun a feasibility study for initiating a Master's Program. It proved compatible with the mission and goals of the Chestnut Hill, which chose a Master of Education Degree with concentration in Elementary and Early Childhood Education. These Undergraduate Programs were well developed; no other college in the area gave such degrees at the time. If college enrollments were on the decline, school enrollments were

on the rise. A Master's Program would service lay teachers, as well as the Sisters of Saint Joseph. Thus it began in the fall of 1980 and enrolled both men and women. Until 1987 Education remained the only Master's Program, directed from 1980 to 1985 by Sister Mary Xavier Kirby who had initiated it before the end of her term as president. It grew slowly, even regressed a bit at the beginning. Eventually it gained strength, and the tortoise is almost outstripping the hare.

The numbers grew from a mere 91 in 1982 to 258 in 1986. By this date, 95 people had earned degrees. Controversial at first, the Graduate Programs gained support from within and without. New programs emerged: in 1987 an M.A./M.S. in Counseling Psychology and Human Services, and in 1990 an M.A. in Holistic Spirituality and Spiritual Direction, developed by future President Sister Carol Vale. Technology in Education, now known as Applied Technology received approval in 1992, through the efforts of Sister Louise Mayock, SND, and Jessica Kahn.

The growing Graduate population brought more students and better income. It also pointed up the need for more space. Classes were in the late afternoon and the evening; more classrooms were thus occupied. Lounge space for nontraditional students was virtually nonexistent, and office space was limited until the late nineties. But good-spirited and hardworking, the

Graduate staff, administration, and faculty remained undaunted, and continued to attract students and devise new ideas.

Among the innovations in the Graduate Division in the eighties were special summer programs, some sponsored and funded for teachers by the School District of Philadelphia and the National Science Foundation. The concentration in Counseling Psychology co-sponsored a major conference "The Family in Crisis: The Real Cost of Addictions" along with Valley Forge Medical Center in 1985, and gave a summer workshop in 1986 on addictions in the marketplace. These and other such workshops and seminars brought people to campus, and they in turn influenced family and friends to come. They especially praised the quality of instruction, individual attention, and the beautiful campus.

The Graduate Division had many distinctive leaders, although their tenure was short. Sister J. Roberta Rivello succeeded Sister Mary Xavier Kirby in 1985, and contributed new programs and creative ideas for courses. Kathleen Rex Anderson became special assistant in 1990 while continuing to work for her doctorate. She helped the program to grow and began negotiations for the Doctor of Psychology. Caroline Golab became Graduate dean in 1993, and was a positive force in directing the energy of faculty and students. She had a caring touch, initiating graduate dinners, affirming faculty and staff, and reorganizing space. When Dr. Golab became dean of the College in 1995, Eugene Kole, OFM Conv., a person of tremendous energy, succeeded her. In 1997, Sister Mary Anne Celenza, a good listener, a compassionate and well-organized person, took over the direction of the division which continues to expand. The Graduate Program numbers about six hundred students who provide a vibrant addition to the College.

While the Education Program grew from the undergraduate degree, Counseling Psychology was independent from the beginning. The College administration supported the professional activities of the professors, many of whom taught in the Undergraduate Division. Composed of seven full-time faculty members and some fifteen adjuncts in 1999, the department offers adolescent psychological assessment, object relationships, play therapy, and life-span development. Specializations in the program have developed from these orientations. While Addictions Counseling was once very popular, child and adolescent therapy is fast moving to the lead.

Counseling Psychology reached a peak on April 25, 1997. After four years of preparation begun with the department, and with the encouragement of the president, the Psy.D. Degree was approved. A clinical program based on a practitioner model, it admits from sixteen to twenty candidates a year, mainly from people already practicing in the field. Psychological Assessment is the most popular concentration. The program normally takes from four to six years, and is unique in that the candidates move through it together. It also offers small classes, flexible scheduling, and the opportunity to develop a professional network with the creation of a community of learners. Candidates will complete their studies in research or clinical analysis culminating in a dissertation. The Psy.D. Program plans to seek accreditation from the American Psychological Association as soon as it is eligible.

If Counseling Psychology is the most popular degree program, Holistic Spirituality and Spiritual Direction is one of the most unusual. It attracts people of various religious traditions, who wish to explore the spiritual life in a holistic manner. Many applicants began to delve into the roots of Christian spirituality and discover an important role for spiritual direction. A collaborative D.Min. Program in conjunction with the Lutheran Seminary brings their students to Chestnut Hill. Eventually Chestnut Hill hopes to establish its own D.Min. Degree and is currently exploring the possibilities.

A special focus in the spirituality program is Health and Spirituality, funded by Dr. Rosalie Reardon Albers, '39. She was grateful to her two schools, Chestnut Hill for giving her a moral and spiritual focus, and the Medical College of Pennsylvania (formerly Women's Medical College) for her medical training, and funded a program for both that would focus on spirituality and ethics in the medical profession. Sister Roseann Quinn, chair of the Religious Studies Department, is exploring ways of incorporating such courses in the curricula of medical schools, and at the same time considering a certificate or a degree program in Spirituality and Healing.

Like the ACCELERATED program, the Graduate Division is also expanding and hopes to meet the twenty-first century with new degrees. Administration of Human Services, Mediation Studies, Liberal Studies, Spirituality and Healing, and a reintroduction of the M.Ed. in Educational Leadership are closest to implementation. Certification programs are being developed in Educational Leadership, Instructional Technology Specialist, and Spirituality and Healing. The Graduate Division is considering off-campus sites, in programs leading to a B.S./M.S. in the Psychology and Education specialties. Doctoral programs in Ministry and Educational Leadership will complete the immediate agenda. With success and new demands, more and greater proposals will inevitably emerge.

Students come to Chestnut Hill for their graduate degrees for much the same reasons as in the College for Women and ACCELERATED. Primarily, they are persons here, not numbers. Teachers know their names and give them personal attention. Classes are small; people can express their ideas. Here they will imbibe principles and morals as well as knowledge. Their teachers are active practitioners in their field. If a student comes for advice or help, someone is always available.

Today Chestnut Hill exists for far more than the traditional young woman: it includes men in its ACCELERATED and Graduate Division; it invites women of all ages through the College for Women. It welcomes everyone. It is open to all religions, as it was in 1924, while maintaining its Catholic identity. It actively seeks all races and cultures, as it did when Sister Maria Kostka first sought to bring students from abroad to campus in the early thirties. It welcomes students from all economic levels, among them those in need, true to the mission of the Sisters of St. Joseph and the example of the Depression days when the College was commended for its financial aid. It professes a service orientation, the social conscience as strong as in the twenties.

Chestnut Hill College in 1999 is not alone in these characteristics. A study done by Sister Kathryn Miller in 1993–1994 of the twelve colleges in the SSJ Consortium[63] reveals that all are known first of all as caring communities. They exist to promote the dignity and worth of every human person without distinction, from the eighteen-year-old scholarship winner, to the single parent, to the professional, to the senior citizen. They address the needs of the times, as soon as they can. They strive for excellence in everything from academics to support services. Finally, they make a difference in the local and world community. Students come and leave with a desire to improve society. In the company of other colleges that hark back to 1650, to 1836, to the early twentieth century when Catholic higher education for women blossomed, Chestnut Hill will greet the new millennium faithful to the tradition of its goals and mission, yet willing to risk the future.

181

Three presidents, from left, Sisters Matthew Anita MacDonald, Mary Xavier Kirby, and Carol Jean Vale come together in the Rotunda

CHAPTER FOURTEEN
INTO THE THIRD MILLENNIUM

O College and Teachers and We
A Loyal Trinity. . . .

O College:

When the twentieth century was young, the College was a dream. It was to be Mount St. Joseph on the Wissahickon; it would be the culmination of years of teaching by the Sisters of St. Joseph. In 1924 it received a name; it was real. In 1928 it had a "local habitation," a grandiose new building, one of the finest in academic architecture. Of Olympic stature, Fournier Hall stood atop the hill recalling the traditions of Umbrian romanesque and signaling the risks of a new venture. Would students fill its halls? Would they move out into the world from the guarded fortress on the hill as educated leaders? Would the first anchor in time and space see other satellites around it?

Time and space are but the externals; the dream incarnated in reality took on spirit. It was the spirit of 1650, when women consecrated to God began to prove to an incredulous world that they too could serve others, and that the cloister was no more than love of God and all human persons. It was the spirit of 1794, when women valued their mission to the extent that they died for it. It was the spirit of Lyon, of refoundation, of rebirth, of reanimation. It was the pioneer spirit that crossed an ocean and a continent to come to an obscure estate near a skeptical town, to found Mount St. Joseph.

The walls of the new College imbibed these traditions and risks, and added others. This adventure in academia saw determination. The College *would* be accredited, albeit five months before the first graduates were to receive their degrees. It *would* be rec-

---

THE MISSION OF CHESTNUT HILL COLLEGE

is to provide students with holistic education in an inclusive Catholic community marked by academic excellence, shared responsibility, personal and professional growth, service to one another and to the global community, and concern for the Earth.

CHESTNUT HILL COLLEGE

9601 Germantown Avenue
Philadelphia, PA 19118-2693
215.248.7000
www.chc.edu

---

ognized by the finest professional associations in the country, even after five, ten, fifteen years of effort. It *would* hold its own among its competitors, from athletics to academics. It would be filled with able women who could face the world confidently, armed with a Mount St. Joseph diploma. It would stand for Judaeo-Christian values, for a social conscience, for excellence in liberal arts.

What was a risk for 1924 and 1928 is tradition in 1999. Fournier did stand; students did come; graduates poured out into the country and the world. The sparkling new structure of 1928 saw a Library and a Residence Hall surround it in 1962. It looks forward to yet another satellite: the Barbara Martino Hall that will blend into a unified campus, bringing openness and light to the citadel on the hill. Once again, time and space will take on flesh, and another monument will articulate the human spirit and architectural potential. Fournier will transform its vigor of 1928 to the idiom of the twenty-first century, and technology will propel it into the future.

Risks there were, and risks there still will be. Costs were high in 1928; they are higher seventy-five years later. Chestnut Hill was never rich; its tradition allies it with all social classes. Yet it has friends. From Murtha Quinn in 1928 to the 1980s Capital Campaign,

185

Under a rare March snowfall the College Administration participate in groundbreaking for Martino Hall.

Michelle Lesher and Julie Fertsch, '00, Student Government leaders, enjoy the College and project the future.

to the mid-1990s Capital Gifts Initiative, to the alumnae gifts throughout the years, to Ann and Hal Sorgenti in 1998, to Barbara and Rocco Martino in 1999, it sees money expand to the point of financing new projects. It also has devoted leaders who work to bring plans and finances together, from Mother Mary James Rogers and Sister Maria Kostka Logue who launched Fournier and the College, to Sister Catharine Frances Redmond who built Fontbonne and Logue Library, to Sister Mary Xavier Kirby who created innovative programs, to Sister Matthew Anita MacDonald who renovated the science and athletic facilities, to Sister Carol Vale who brings the dream of another new structure into being.

And Teachers:

Listen quietly as you walk along the hushed corridors of Fournier and St. Joseph's Hall; you will hear familiar voices. Step into what is now the ACCELERATED Office; you will hear Sister Clare Joseph giving you explicit directions on filling in your roster. Look across the hall; you will hear a card game in process, and one person who has to win. Sister Maria Kostka had to win with the College, it had to be the best, and you will see her relentlessly working for thirty years in the office down the corridor. Move into Clement Hall; you will hear Sister Maria

Walburg bring immortal Rome to life. You will hear Dr. Gergely preparing future teachers, or Dr. Walsh lecture on philosophy. "Mademoiselle" will invite you to "devil-up" your idea, and just "sink." Sister Jane Frances will whirl you through math with a piece of chalk in one hand and an eraser in another. Move to the Assembly Room, and you will find Miss Gow bringing the best of poetry and drama to an audience able to appreciate it only later. Come into the Music Corridor in St. Joseph's Hall, and you will sing and play with Sister Regina Dolores. Climb to the fifth floor, and you will draw and design with Sister Mary Julia; you will tackle science experiments with Sisters Eleanor Marie and Miriam Elizabeth.

Wait a little longer, and you will hear other voices. Sister Helen de Sales will show you what social justice really means, and Sister Catharine Frances will direct you to the inner city where you can practice it. Miss Corcoran will develop your social graces and invite you to explore Europe with her. Go to the gym and Miss Buckley will help you to be physically fit, and to compete in the world of sports, no matter what your ability is. Go to class and Dr. Lukacs and Sister Consuelo Maria will make you a part of History. Father Lynch will make Literature come alive for you, "gurrl." You will see Fashion Design models come down the aisle under Sister Stella Bernard's imaginative direction. You will learn the trees of the campus with Sister Paul Daniel, and the secrets of Chemistry from Sister Patrick Marie.

Most of these voices are hushed now; none are heard on campus today. Yet their presence remains. They, along with many others, are the great teachers who have marked the minds and memories of thousands of graduates. They were competent and exciting; they worked to be the best in their fields. Yet something else marks them as truly Chestnut Hill teachers. They took a personal interest in each and every student. They were as concerned over her love traumas as her course problems. They always took the extra minute, or hour, or day that it needed to respond. They urged each and every one to be the very best that she could do and be. They will never be forgotten.

In 1999 there are fewer sisters on campus, while the number of lay people has grown. Yet the same spirit still prevails. Whether a student comes to the College for Women, ACCELERATED, or the Graduate Program, teachers are still the best they can be in their fields, and they incite their students to the same quality of excellence. These professors of the twenty-first century are still interested in their students. They know each one by name, and they will help the person academically or personally. Chestnut Hill will continue to need more such faculty members, people who stress values, social concerns, and excellence. Most of all it will need people with the personal touch, because of whom the student can believe that he or she really matters.

And We. . . .

We, the students, the graduates, the seven thousand alumnae/i, we complete the loyal trinity, from the fifteen fledgling ladies, who with many additions and subtractions made up the Class of 1928 to the several hundred graduates from all three divisions who crowd under the tent on a May afternoon. Without "us," the students, there would be no college. A building sets the stage, a faculty directs the drama, but only if the actors perform will there truly be life. And perform they did: in the games and clubs of the twenties, in the May Days and publications of the thirties, in the war efforts and Bond Nights of the forties, in the aquacades and operas of the fifties, in the revolts and Arts Festivals of the sixties, in the new programs and shared decisions of the seventies, in the revived traditions and career awareness of the eighties, in the information explosion and strategic vision of the nineties.

Students took risks which became traditions: witness the first Christmas tree in the sisters' community room and you will see the special uniqueness of every Christmas. They looked for work when there was none in the Depression, and moved into Science and Technology during the war and after it. They crafted words to express their ideas, and chose Mithridates as their spokesperson. They recorded history faithfully in the thirty-eight years of *Fournier News*, and used *One Small Voice* and *Kaleidoscope* to give their opinions. They answered the cries of the needy and the poor in Philadelphia, North Carolina, Central America. They became leaders. And yes, they studied.

The campus of 1924 and 1934 and even 1944 was home. Activities centered around school. These were the golden years of clubs and dances, of concerts and plays. Few owned cars; permissions were minimal. A homogeneous student body enjoyed one another and brought their male friends to campus. The end of the war brought mobility and diversity; cars and a new population. It brought more security and earlier marriages. It invited complacency, which would be shattered in the winds of the sixties. Suddenly there was no longer a captive audience on the hill; women could attend former "men only" colleges. The answers of the fifties no longer applied to the sixties. With revolt came alienation, short-lived, but real. A job became as important as an education.

185

The seventies and eighties saw fewer young women choosing Chestnut Hill, but they saw a changed population: ethnically diverse, varied in age, and even brought men to campus. These were years of searching, questioning, recruiting. Women still came; they still saw a role for single-sex education; they too became leaders and joined the loyal ranks of the alumnae. But look at the campus of 1999. It enrolls over sixteen hundred students, men, women, old, young, white, Asian, Hispanic, African American, Christian, Jewish, Muslim: truly diverse. It is alive and growing. While the College for

Women preserves its identity, true to the traditions of the twenties, it is not alone. Nor can it stand alone.

Chestnut Hill has always aimed to address the needs of the day. Women will always need special attention, "for on the education of women depends the future of society." Even though ACCELERATED and the Graduate Division are co-ed, the focus is on women. The College community continues to explore just what this will mean for the twenty-first century, and in the question is the solution. In 2024 the composition of the College may be different, but if "College and Teachers and We" remain true to the spirit of 1924, of 1847, of 1650, there will be a dynamic, involved, competent student body, ready to assume leadership in the world of tomorrow. They will learn to make a living, because they must, but most of all they will certainly learn how to live.

It is only by dreaming that one can touch reality. The dream of 1904, come to being in 1924, turns to the new millennium. Once again, there are dreams: a large building, an impressive athletic center, more athletes who are also scholars. Aging dorms look for new life. Computers, the internet, e-mail can come into them and network throughout the campus with the help of the new generator. A modern boiler system will assure climate control. New roofing will keep the revered buildings dry and safe for another seventy-five years. Perhaps even the parking problems will be solved.

Teachers dream of an ideal curriculum, local and global experiences, new majors, new life in old ones. They envision more minors, more options, a combined B.S./M.S in five years, distance learning. The Graduate Program projects additional Master's and Doctoral Degrees. Teachers also dream of time and money for enrichment, the completion of a research project, exploration of new ideas. They hope for greater financial security, so that they can remain the guide and helper for tomorrow's students.

Students dream of adequate space, of comfortable apartment-like rooms, of better security. They dream of a spot that will be uniquely theirs, where campus life can flourish. They hope for suitable campus employment. They would like state-of-the art classrooms, with a learner-centered focus. Graduate students also would like a place on campus, and lounges of their own. All would like to see numbers increase, in a climate of geographic and ethnic diversity, with new recruits committed to the spirit and traditions of the College, willing to prepare for careers of leadership in a yet uncharted future. They want to be leaders not only for professional advancement, but for service as well, as they have been taught since the College first began.

Will these dreams come to pass? Will they be reality in 2004, in 2024? If there is the same determination that directed our forebears in 1904 and 1924, they will. If selfless people believe in a mission, and are committed to Judaeo-Christian values, risks will once again become traditions. It was because "College and Teachers and We" believed in the future that they moved forward together to create a forum for truth and beauty, a path to leadership and scholarship, and an atmosphere to develop mind, body, and spirit. They forged ahead fearlessly; risks were the material that wove the fabric of success, and it is on our traditions that we face a new century of risks.

Our hearts' deep fealty
Is pledged unto thee,
Is pledged unto thee,
Our loved Chestnut Hill!

Barbara Martino Hall as it appeared in August of 1999.

The architect's computer projection of the Barbara Martino Convocation/Communications Center and the court that will unite it, St. Joseph's Hall and Fournier Hall.

The architect's computer projection of the new Center as seen from Northwestern Avenue.

SELECTED BIBLIOGRAPHY

Selected Books

Alumnae/i Directory 1996, Chestnut Hill College. White Plains,
  N.Y.: Bernard C. Harris Publishing Company, 1996.

Bois, Chanoine A. Les Soeurs de Saint-Joseph, Filles du Petit
  Dessin. Lyon: Imprimeries du Sud-Est, 1950.

Buckley, Betty. Sixty Years of Sports at Chestnut Hill College
  1924–1984. Chestnut Hill College, 1984.

Contosta, David R. Suburb in the City: Chestnut Hill,
  Philadelphia, 1850–1990. Columbus: Ohio
  University Press, 1992.

____. Villanova University, 1842–1992. University Park:
  Pennsylvania State University, 1995.

Furniss, W. Todd and Graham, Patricia Albjerg. Women in
  Higher Education. Washington D.C.: American
  Council on Education, 1974.

Gouit, F. Les Soeurs de Saint-Joseph du Puy-en-Velay,
  1648–1915. Le Puy: Imprimerie de l'Avenir de la
  Haute-Loire, 1930.

Logue, Sister Maria Kostka. Sisters of St. Joseph of
  Philadelphia. Westminster, Maryland: The Newman
  Press, 1950.

Lukacs, John. A Sketch of the History of Chestnut Hill College,
  1924–1974. Chestnut Hill College, 1975.

Manory, RoseMarie. Of Glory, Of Praise: A 75-Year History of
  The College of Saint Rose. Albany: The College of St.
  Rose, 1994.

Oates, Mary J., ed. Higher Education for Catholic Women. New
  York and London: Garland Publishing, Inc., 1987.

Power, Edward J. A History of Catholic Higher Education in the
  United States. Milwaukee: The Bruce Publishing
  Company, 1958.

Savage, Sister Mary Lucida. The Congregation of Saint Joseph
  of Carondelet. St. Louis: B. Herder Book Company,
  1923.

Solomon, Barbara Miller. In the Company of Educated Women.
  New Haven and London: Yale University Press,
  1985.

Selected Manuscripts, Articles, and Interviews

Bennis, Sister Ann Edward. "An Unpredictable SSJ."
  Unpublished, 1960.

College Catalogues.

Contosta, David. "Life at Immaculata, Rosemont, and
  Chestnut Hill: 1920–1975." Publication pending.

Faculty Meeting Minutes, Chestnut Hill College.

Kashuba, Sister Mary Helen. Interviews of Sisters Mary Julia
  Daly, Consuelo Maria Aherne, Mary Xavier Kirby,
  Roseann Quinn; Kathleen Rex Anderson, Scott
  Browning.

Miller, Sister Kathryn. "The SSJ College Consortium, Mission
  and Image." Occasional Papers on Catholic Higher
  Education. ACCU, I, 2, December 1995.

Rafferty, Sister Grace Margaret. Interviews of Sisters Mary
  Julia Daly, Consuelo Maria Aherne, Rita Madeleine
  Gruber, Harriet P. Corrigan, Patrick Marie Flood;
  John Lukacs, Freda Gorelick Oben, Elizabeth
  Rafferty, Eleanore Dolan Egan.

Reports of Registrars, Deans, Presidents.

Self-Study Reports, Chestnut Hill College.

Smith, Sister Marie de Sales. "Chestnut Hill College Campus."
  Unpublished, 1967.

____. "The First Mount Saint Joseph College." Unpublished,
  1970.

____. "History of Mount Saint Joseph Academy."
  Unpublished, 1972.

Principal Newspapers and Magazines

Alumnae Bulletin, Chestnut Hill College.
Ambler Gazette, The.
Aurelian, Chestnut Hill College.
Catholic Standard and Times, The.
Chestnut Hill Local, The.
Fournier News, Chestnut Hill College.
Fourth Estate, Chestnut Hill College.
Germantown Courier, The.
Grackle, The, Chestnut Hill College.
Hill, The, Chestnut Hill College.
Kaleidoscope, Chestnut Hill College.
MS. Magazine.
New York Times, The.
Newsweek Magazine.
Philadelphia Bulletin, The.
Philadelphia Inquirer, The.
Time Magazine.

Archives

Archives of the Sisters of St. Joseph, Mt. St. Joseph Convent.
Archives of Chestnut Hill College
Chestnut Hill Historical Society, The.
Germantown Historical Society, The.
Office of Publicity, Chestnut Hill College.

ENDNOTES

1. Archives of the Sisters of St. Joseph, hereafter
referred to as ASSJ.

2. A. Bois, Les Soeurs de Saint-Joseph. (Lyon: Editions
et Impimerie du Sud-Est, 1950) 230.

3. Sister M. Lucida Savage, CSJ. History of the Sisters of
St. Joseph of Carondelet. (St. Louis: Herder, 1923) 51.

4. Sister Maria Kostka Logue, Sisters of St. Joseph of
Philadelphia (Westminster: The Newman Press, 1950) 95.

5. Logue, 163.

6. Logue, 169.

7. Logue, 169.

8. Sister Marie de Sales Smith, "Chestnut Hill College
Campus." Unpublished, 1967.

9. Logue, 98.

10. Chestnut Hill College Archives, hereafter referred to
as CHCA.

11. ASSJ.

12. Logue, 207.

13. Sister Marie de Sales Smith, "The First Mount Saint
Joseph College." Unpublished, 1970, 8.

14. Sister Marie de Sales Smith, "History of Mount St.
Joseph Academy. Unpublished.

15. Smith, "The First Mount," 2.

16. Barbara Miller Solomon, In the Company of Educated
Women (New Haven and London: Yale University Press, 1985):
16.

17. Solomon, 145.

18. CHCA. Further correspondence comes from this
source.

19. John Lukacs, A Sketch of the History of Chestnut Hill
College, 1924–1974 (Chestnut Hill College, 1975) 10.

20. Betty Buckley, Sixty Years of Sports at Chestnut Hill
College 1924–1984 (Chestnut Hill College, 1985) 1–4.

21. The other bidders and their conditions were: John
McShain: $1,059,987; Murphy-Quigley: $1,100,000; completed by August 1, 1928; Doyle and Company: $1,134,800; com-
pleted by December 31, 1928; F. V. Warren: $1,149,715; com-
pleted by December 1, 1928; and Frank G. Stewart:
$1,162,520; completed in eighteen months. ASSJ.

22. Sister Ann Edward Bennis, "An Unpredictable SSJ."
Unpublished, 1960, 18.

23. Interview of Sister Consuelo Maria Aherne by Sister
Grace Margaret Rafferty. Transcript of a tape, 1985, 7.

24. Logue, 77.

25. Class history, Class of 1928, CHCA.

26. President's Report, June 30, 1938. Statistics compiled by Sister Catherine Frances. CHCA.

27. Lukacs, 13.

28. Lukacs, 12–13.

29. E. J. Gergely, Student Teachers Bulletin 9 (May
1939): 15.

30. College Catalogue, 1935–1936: 12.

31. Buckley, 42.

32. David R. Contosta, "Life at Immaculata, Rosemont,
and Chestnut Hill: 1920–1975." Publication pending.

33. Logue, 279.

34. Lukacs, 14.

35. Fournier News 12:1(October 9, 1942): 2.

36. Logue, 268.

37. Letter from Sister M. Francisca, the Mary Guild, Cornwells Heights, to Sister Catharine Frances, December 3, 1937. ACHC.

38. Recollections of Mariagnes O'Neill Brown.

39. Buckley, 50.

40. Interview of Sister Mary Julia Daly by Sister Grace Margaret Rafferty, October 8, 1985. CHCA.

41. Interview of John Lukacs by Sister Grace Margaret Rafferty, November 20, 1985.

42. See *The Chestnut Hill Local*, July 28, 1960, and the *Philadelphia Bulletin* for July 20, 1960.

43. *Fournier News*, October 12, 1961.

44. Dorothy Barton, memoirs. CHCA.

45. *The Inquirer*, March 10, 1971. See a similar article in *The Bulletin*.

46. Letter to Sister Mary Xavier from Kristine McGowan, State Coordinator—Act 101, December 12, 1974.

47. Solomon, Chapter 7.

48. Since 1969, the Board of Trustees was known as the Board of Directors, considered a more appropriate description of their function.

49. Lukacs, 45; see also *The Sunday Bulletin*, June 25, 1975, for this and other similar experiences.

50. Article by Marie Jones, September 28, 1967.

51. Buckley, 7.

52. In addition, Anne Marie Tate, '69, and Joanna Rizzo, '72, were daughters of sitting mayors of Philadelphia.

53. Sister Mary Xavier, Retirement Party for Sister Jane Frances, June 24, 1992.

54. This was not because of dissatisfaction on either side, but rather because the State would soon require a B.S. degree in Nursing.

55. *The Fourth Estate*, editorial, December 1984.

56. Patricia Canning Kalinowsky, '70, "President Enriches College's Heritage; Leaves Enduring Legacy." *The Hill* (Summer 1992): 13. Much other information about the Capital Campaign comes from this article.

57. Middle States Self-Study Report (1991) 6.18.

58. See research by Georgia McWhinney, Ph.D. in the Self-Study Report for 1991, A.1.

59. Self-Study, 9.2.

60. Interview by Joanne Ahearne, "A New President Defining Roots and Mission," *The Hill* (Spring 1993).

61. *Periodic Review*, 1997.

62. See listings in Middle States Reports, *The Hill*, and the programs for the Opening Convocations.

63. Kathryn Miller, SSJ. "The SSJ College Consortium: Mission and Image." *Occasional Papers on Catholic Higher Education.* ACCCU I (December 1995):2.

INDEX

ABOUT THE AUTHOR

Mary Helen Kashuba, SSJ, DML, is currently professor of French and Russian at Chestnut Hill College in Philadelphia, Pennsylvania, where she has taught since 1963. She received her A.B. from Chestnut Hill College, her M.A. from Fordham University, and her doctorate from Middlebury College, Vermont. Among her awards are a Fulbright Grant to France, two summer grants to Russia from the International Research and Exchanges Board, the Lindback Award for Distinguished Teaching, and the *Palmes Académiques*, from the French government for out-standing service in French. She has led over fifteen study tours to France and Russia. She is the author of many articles on litera-ture and pedagogy, and has given over thirty presentations at local, national, and international meet-ings of professional associations. She is active in many professional associations, was president of local chapters and was regional repre-sentative of the American Association of Teachers of French from 1990 to 1995. She currently resides at Chestnut Hill College.